6471

DATE DUE

DATE DUE			
FEB 24 1999			
APR 29 1998			

00467-0

974.4   Kent, Deborah
KEN   America the beautiful.
           Massachusetts

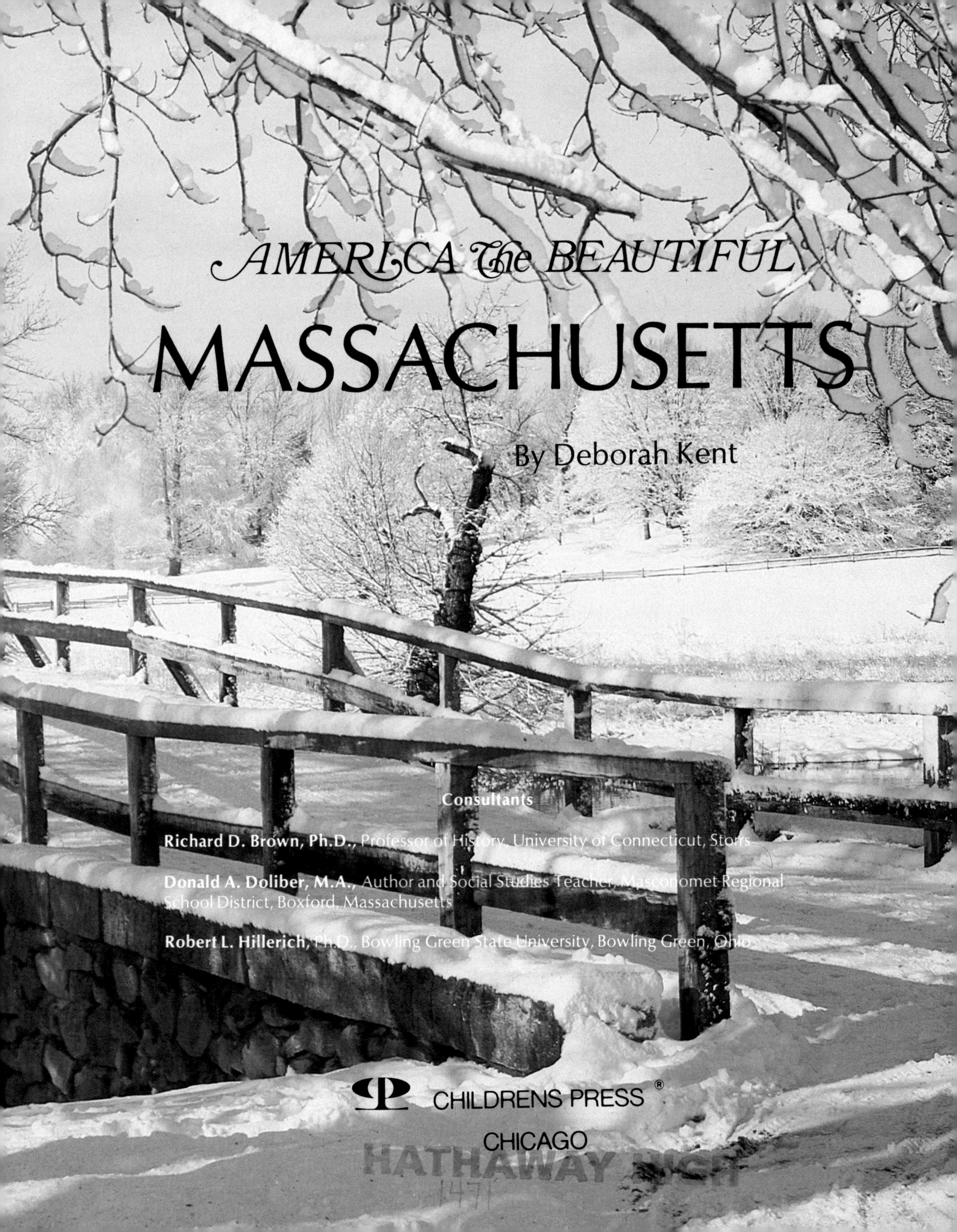

AMERICA the BEAUTIFUL

MASSACHUSETTS

By Deborah Kent

Consultants

Richard D. Brown, Ph.D., Professor of History, University of Connecticut, Storrs

Donald A. Doliber, M.A., Author and Social Studies Teacher, Masconomet Regional School District, Boxford, Massachusetts

Robert L. Hillerich, Ph.D., Bowling Green State University, Bowling Green, Ohio

CHILDRENS PRESS®

CHICAGO

Boston's Faneuil Hall (center) at night

Project Editor: Joan Downing
Assistant Editor: Shari Joffe
Design Director: Margrit Fiddle
Typesetting: Graphic Connections, Inc.
Engraving: Liberty Photoengraving

Childrens Press®, Chicago
Copyright ©1987 by Regensteiner Publishing Enterprises, Inc.
All rights reserved. Published simultaneously in Canada.
Printed in the United States of America.
    4 5 6 7 8 9 10 R 96 95 94 93 92 91

Library of Congress Cataloging-in-Publication Data

Kent, Deborah.
    America the beautiful, Massachusetts.

    (America the beautiful state books)
    Includes index.
    Summary: Introduces the geography, history,
government, economy, industry, culture, historic sites,
and famous people of this historically significant
state.
    1.   Massachusetts—Juvenile literature.
[1.   Massachusetts]   I.   Title.   II.   Series.
F64.3.K46   1987   974.4   87-9402
ISBN 0-516-00467-0

A roadside vegetable stand in central Massachusetts

TABLE OF CONTENTS

Chapter 1

WHERE PAST AND FUTURE MEET

WHERE PAST AND FUTURE MEET

On a sunny morning in early June, four cows clamber down a
wooden ramp from a large van onto the Boston Common. Ears
twitching nervously, they gaze at the level carpet of green
bordered by a steady stream of roaring traffic. After a moment,
one cow lowers her head and begins to crop the grass at her feet.

The oldest city park in the nation, the Boston Common was set
aside in 1634 as public grazing land. Today, a nearly forgotten law
permitting Bostonians to graze their cattle on the green remains
on the books. In keeping with this tradition, the city brings a
small herd of cows to the Common during National Dairy Week.
Thousands of urban schoolchildren are given their first glimpse of
real cows. A few even get to try their hand at milking.

The people of Massachusetts have an enduring respect for
tradition, taking pride in their state's key role in America's
history. From Boston to the tiniest town, the visitor finds restored
colonial homes, working models of early factories, and museums
crammed with priceless documents.

Today, on the very streets where colonists once walked, men
and women work at the forefront of modern technology.
Massachusetts' universities and research centers draw some of the
finest minds in the country to make dramatic advances in
medicine, computers, and communications. Yet as they reach
toward the future, the people of Massachusetts cherish their ties to
the past and keep their traditions alive. On some June mornings,
cows still walk on the Boston Common, a reminder to a new
generation of children of how their state began more than three
centuries ago.

Chapter 2
THE LAND

THE LAND

Some twenty thousand years ago, a vast sheet of ice crept down from the earth's polar region until it covered the land known today as Massachusetts. The great glacier scraped away layers of topsoil, fractured the earth's crust, and tossed chunks of bedrock to the surface. Then, the ice receded as slowly as it had come, leaving a scarred and pitted landscape in its wake.

Little by little the land restored itself. Forests took root on rocky hillsides, and animals and birds flourished. Early English settlers wrote glowing accounts of forests that were thick with wild fruit and game. But the glacier left its legacy in the rough, stony soil that defied the farmer's plow. The harshness of the land has shaped the history of Massachusetts and the character of the people who make it their home.

GEOGRAPHY AND TOPOGRAPHY

Most of Massachusetts forms a narrow rectangle, its boundaries set by surveyors with little regard for natural landmarks such as rivers and mountains. Nature takes over on the Atlantic Coast, however, and the eastern end of the oblong is ragged with capes and bays. The nickname "Bay State" comes from Massachusetts Bay, which stretches from Cape Ann in the north to Plymouth in the south. From the southeastern corner of the state, Cape Cod

The Massachusetts landscape is extremely varied, encompassing rocky coastland (above), lush forests (right), sandy beaches, fertile farmland, rolling hills, and even mountains.

reaches 65 miles (105 kilometers) into the ocean like a great, outthrust arm.

Massachusetts is one of six northeastern states that make up the region called New England. To its north lie New Hampshire and Vermont, while Connecticut and Rhode Island border it to the south. New York, not part of New England, is its western neighbor.

Covering 8,284 square miles (21,456 square kilometers), Massachusetts ranks forty-fifth in size among the states. Only New Jersey, Connecticut, Hawaii, Delaware, and Rhode Island are smaller. From north to south, the state's longest distance is 110 miles (177 kilometers). The greatest distance from east to west is 190 miles (306 kilometers) and can be traveled in about three hours by car. But this short drive carries the visitor from wooded hills in the west, through the fertile Connecticut Valley, to the sparkling beaches of Cape Cod. Small though it is, Massachusetts offers a landscape of surprising variety.

A HERITAGE OF THE SEA

Some Massachusetts houses built in port towns early in the
nineteenth century were crowned by a widow's walk, a narrow
gallery overlooking the ocean. Legend says that the wives of
sailors, sometimes left alone for years at a time, would pace along
their widow's walks day after day, gazing out in search of an
approaching ship.

From the earliest days of European settlement, the ocean has
had far-reaching effects on Massachusetts life. Massachusetts'
192-mile (309-kilometer) coastline is scored with fine natural
harbors that set the stage for the state's prominence in shipping
and fishing. Today Massachusetts' beaches are a magnet for
summer tourists who flee Eastern cities to find surf and sunshine.

In 1824, poet Felicia Hemans described the shore of
Massachusetts as "a stern and rock-bound coast." Much of the
coast is still a forbidding tumble of glacial boulders. Yet the
granite coves of Cape Ann and the harbor at Salem have a stark
beauty all their own.

While the northern portion of the coast was molded by the
great glacier, Cape Cod was created by the gradual work of the
pounding sea. Over thousands of years, the ocean currents heaped
vast drifts of sand against a ridge of glacial debris, forming a
narrow, ever-shifting peninsula. The low-lying land is especially
vulnerable to storms. At Provincetown, on the Cape's farthest tip,
old-timers like to say that "the village covers the waterfront when
the waterfront doesn't cover the village."

South of the Cape lie two sandy islands that are both roughly
triangular in shape. Nantucket covers about 65 square miles
(168 square kilometers); Martha's Vineyard is nearly twice that
size. Northwest of Martha's Vineyard cluster the sixteen tiny

Both the natural harbor at Gloucester (above) and the island of Martha's Vineyard (right) were formed by a great glacier that covered Massachusetts during the Ice Age.

Elizabeth Islands, named for England's Queen Elizabeth I by early British explorers.

The offshore islands and the eastern third of the Massachusetts mainland are known collectively as the Coastal Lowlands. On the mainland, the region extends westward some 30 miles (48 kilometers). Here and there rise low, rounded hills—mounds of debris left behind by the glacier. The most striking of these is the Great Blue Hill near Quincy, once home to a group of Indians called the Massachusett, who took their name from the word they used to describe the hill. The early British settlers in turn gave the name to the colony they founded in the New World. Thus Massachusetts means, literally, "near the great hill."

THE UPLAND AND THE VALLEY

As one travels away from the coast, the land rises gradually to form a belt of low, rocky hills. This area is part of a land region known as the Eastern New England Upland. The stony soil here is a constant disappointment to the farmer. But the swift-flowing streams that tumble through this region provide waterpower for many of the state's factories.

Farther to the west, the land slopes down again to the Connecticut Valley. The Connecticut River, the longest river to flow through Massachusetts, deposits a rich cargo of silt as it rolls from New Hampshire into Connecticut. Consequently, this region, known as the Connecticut Valley Lowland, contains the state's most productive farmland. At towns such as Springfield and Holyoke, the Connecticut River has been harnessed for industrial development.

THE BERKSHIRE HILLS

Beyond the Connecticut Valley the land rises sharply once more. Within thirty miles (forty-eight kilometers) one comes upon the Berkshire Hills, which offer some of the loveliest scenery in all of Massachusetts. The Berkshires are included in a land region called the Western New England Upland, which stretches through Vermont, Massachusetts, and Connecticut. At the westernmost edge of the state lies a tiny section of the Taconic Mountains, a range that extends through much of New York and into Vermont. A ten-mile- (sixteen-kilometer-) wide strip of fertile lowland between the Berkshires and the Taconic Mountains is known as the Berkshire Valley.

In dramatic contrast to the low plain along the coast, the Berkshires average some 2,000 feet (610 meters) in height. Mount Greylock, the highest point in the state, towers 3,491 feet (1,064 meters) above sea level. With their long, steep slopes, the Berkshires enjoy a booming ski season each winter.

RIVERS AND LAKES

Massachusetts is crisscrossed by 4,230 miles (6,006 kilometers) of rivers and streams, most of these relatively small. The longest and most important river is the Connecticut River, which cuts across the state on its way from New Hampshire to Connecticut. The Connecticut's many tributaries include the Deerfield, Westfield, Millers, and Chicopee rivers. The scenic Housatonic River winds south through the Berkshires. The Merrimack is the chief river of the Coastal Lowlands, forming the eastern portion of the Massachusetts-New Hampshire border. The Charles and the Mystic empty into Boston Harbor.

Massachusetts is dotted with more than thirteen hundred tiny lakes and ponds, many of which were carved out by the great glacier. The largest body of fresh water in the state is the man-made Quabbin Reservoir in the Eastern Upland. Covering 39 square miles (101 square kilometers), the Quabbin is one of the largest artificial reservoirs in the nation, and is the chief water source for metropolitan Boston.

The Massachusetts coast is rich with marine life. Collecting edible clams called quahogs (left) and going on whale-watches (above) are two popular coastal activities.

PLANT AND ANIMAL LIFE

Though Massachusetts is one of the nation's most industrial states, three-fifths of its land is covered with forests. The woods are thick with hardwoods such as oak, hickory, ash, and maple, and with hemlock, pine, and other evergreens. Among the loveliest of the state's wildflowers are violets, trilliums, and lady's slippers.

In the Berkshires, one of the least-developed areas of the state, travelers may glimpse the flash of a white tail as a deer bounds into the underbrush. The Berkshires are also home to raccoons, skunks, red foxes, and beavers. Every fall, hunters take their quota of grouse, pheasants, and wild ducks.

The Massachusetts coast is rich with marine life. Tons of clams, soft-shell crabs, and lobster are harvested each year. Schools of codfish, flounder, and bluefin tuna swarm offshore. The cod was such a mainstay of Massachusetts' early economy that a wooden carving of it hangs in the State House. The whale, too, played an important role in the state's history, as Nantucket and New

16

Bedford were once the hub of the nation's whaling industry. Today tourists board whale-watching boats at Provincetown to sight playful humpbacks or rare right and sei whales.

CLIMATE

Throughout the year, temperatures along the Massachusetts coast are somewhat warmer than those in the western part of the state. In July, Boston's temperature averages 72° Fahrenheit (22.2° Celsius), compared to an average of 68° Fahrenheit (20° Celsius) in Pittsfield in Berkshire County. Average January readings are 29° Fahrenheit (minus 1.7° Celsius) in Boston and 21° Fahrenheit (minus 6.1° Celsius) in Pittsfield. Extremes are not uncommon. On August 2, 1975, the mercury soared to 107° Fahrenheit (41.7° Celsius), the highest temperature ever recorded in the state, at Chester and New Bedford. Birch Hill Dam holds the record for the all-time low: a bone-chilling minus 34° Fahrenheit (minus 36.7° Celsius), on January 18, 1957.

Western Massachusetts receives an average of 44 inches (112 centimeters) of rainfall annually; the coast receives about 4 inches (12 centimeters) less. Snowfall in the Berkshires is considerably heavier than it is along the shore. To the delight of skiers, the hills are buried under 55 to 75 inches (140 to 191 centimeters) of snow each winter. The Boston area averages only 42 inches (107 centimeters). In late summer and early fall the coast is sometimes battered by savage hurricanes, and storms that New Englanders call "nor'easters."

Geography and climate draw many distinctions between eastern and western Massachusetts. These differences have made their mark on the history of the state, and still influence the ways in which people live there today.

Chapter 3
THE PEOPLE

THE PEOPLE

And this is good old Boston,
The home of the bean and the cod,
Where the Lowells talk only to the Cabots,
And the Cabots talk only to God.

This old jingle refers to some of the wealthy, upper-crust
families that dominated the economic and intellectual life of
Boston for generations. The Cabots, the Lawrences, the Appletons,
and the Lowells were among the families nicknamed the "Boston
Brahmins" after the elite Brahmin Class of India. Today, though
the Boston Brahmins are still prominent in the Boston financial
world, their power and influence has been diffused among many
ethnic and cultural groups, each a thread in the complex fabric of
Massachusetts.

POPULATION

Though it is only forty-fifth in size, Massachusetts ranks
eleventh among the states in population, claiming 5,737,081
people according to the 1980 census. It is among the most densely
populated, heavily urbanized states in the nation. With an average
of 693 persons per square mile (268 people per square kilometer)
of land, Massachusetts ranks third in population density, exceeded
only by New Jersey and Rhode Island. Ninety percent of all Bay
Staters are classified as urban dwellers—that is, they live in cities

A general market in Boston

or suburbs—and nearly half of the state's population is concentrated within 50 miles (80.5 kilometers) of Boston. Other major metropolitan areas include Worcester, Springfield, and New Bedford.

In the 1970s and 1980s, American industry drifted away from the traditional "smokestack" cities of the Northeast and Midwest to the "sunbelt" states of the South. This trend is reflected in Massachusetts' .8 percent population growth in the decade from 1970 to 1980. During the same period, population in the nation as a whole rose 11.4 percent.

During the 1980s, however, Massachusetts had the lowest unemployment rate among the ten leading industrial states. From the 1950s onward, hundreds of companies relying on highly advanced technology sprang up along Route 128, which traces a long semicircle west of Boston from Gloucester to Quincy. Professionals from all over the country resettled along Route 128 to be near their jobs. Thus, while most of the Bay State's cities were losing population, many suburban communities experienced a boom. Cape Cod also has seen a surge in population, as retirees turn summer cottages into year-round homes.

ETHNIC MASSACHUSETTS

In 1796 the president of Yale University, Timothy Dwight, wrote that the people of Boston "are all descendants of Englishmen, and of course are united by all the great bonds of society—language, religion, government, manners and interests." Although some blacks, Indians, and people of Scottish or French ancestry lived in the state at the time, English settlers and their descendants predominated in Boston and throughout Massachusetts. For the first two hundred years of the state's history, these Anglo-Americans, or "Yankees," set the tone in politics, religion, and education, and considered themselves to be the only "true" Americans.

By the middle of the nineteenth century, however, a flood of newcomers began to challenge Yankee dominance of the state. In the 1840s, a disastrous famine in Ireland sent more than a million Irish men and women to the United States in search of better lives, and hundreds of thousands settled in Massachusetts. French Canadians began arriving in the 1880s. The end of the nineteenth century brought fresh waves of immigration from European countries such as Scandinavia and Germany. During the first half of the twentieth century, large numbers of Italians, as well as Poles, Portuguese, Syrians, Greeks, and Lebanese, came to

The Italians of Boston's North End (left) are an important part of Massachusetts' ethnic mosaic. During the presidency of John F. Kennedy (above), the Boston accent became a familiar sound to most Americans.

Massachusetts. After World War II, many blacks left the South to find jobs in Massachusetts' factories.

Today, people of all cultures live throughout Massachusetts. In the eastern part of the state, however, ethnic enclaves are more apparent—the Italians of Boston's North End, the Irish of Charleston, the Greeks of Lowell, the Portuguese of Fall River and New Bedford. Most of Massachusetts' blacks, who comprise about 4 per cent of the state's total population, live in Boston and nearby cities. There are large black communities in Springfield, New Bedford, and the Boston sections of Roxbury and Dorchester. Boston also has a distinct Chinese community and a sizable Puerto Rican population. About four thousand people in Massachusetts are of Native American descent, many of them living on Cape Cod and Martha's Vineyard. The largest group of new immigrants are French-speaking Canadians. After English, French is the most frequently spoken language in Massachusetts.

LANGUAGE

When Brookline-born John F. Kennedy became president of the United States in 1960, he charmed the nation with his Boston accent. He inspired the public to "renewed vigah" (vigor) and warned of trouble in the island nation of "Cuber" (Cuba). Actually, the speech pattern known as the Boston accent can be heard all over eastern Massachusetts. The letter *r* is added to words that end with a vowel sound such as *a* or *o*. The *r* is omitted when it appears at the end of a word, or when it precedes a consonant in the middle of a word. Thus, a Bostonian pronounces the word corner as though it had no *r*'s: *cawna*. Newcomers like to parody the Boston accent by saying, "Pahk the cah in Hahvad Yahd!" (Park the car in Harvard Yard).

RELIGION

More than half of all Bay Staters are Roman Catholics, most of them of Irish, Italian, or eastern-European descent. Massachusetts is the second-most heavily Catholic state in the nation.

The state's relatively small Jewish population is concentrated in the Boston area. Most Protestant groups are represented in Massachusetts, with the United Church of Christ and the Episcopalian Church being the most prominent. The Congregational Church, a much-modified descendant of the early Puritan sect that founded the Massachusetts Bay Colony, still has many members. Unitarianism gained its first foothold in the United States in Boston in the early 1800s. The Church of Christ, Scientist was founded in Boston in 1879 by Mary Baker Eddy. Her book *Science and Health with Key to the Scriptures* expressed the belief that healing could be brought about by spiritual means explained in the Bible.

POLITICS

In 1972, the nation voted overwhelmingly to re-elect Richard M. Nixon to the presidency. His opponent, liberal Democrat George McGovern, won electoral votes in only two places—the District of

Columbia, and Massachusetts. McGovern's victory is an example of the recent liberalism of a majority of Massachusetts voters.

For the Irish immigrants of the late 1800s, the Democratic Party became an avenue to power in a Yankee establishment. Irish Democratic candidates gradually won more and more offices throughout the state. One of the most colorful Irish politicians in Massachusetts history was James Michael Curley. Curley served as mayor of Boston intermittently between 1914 and 1950, and was governor of the state from 1935 to 1937. Curley's opponents accused him of widespread corruption, including patronage (rewarding friends, relatives, and supporters with well-paying jobs). Yet Curley earned the unflagging devotion of his poor constituents. When he was fined thirty thousand dollars for fraud in 1938, his loyal followers raised most of the money.

From the 1920s through the 1950s, Democrats and Republicans were about equally represented among Massachusetts congressmen. But from 1928 through 1976, Massachusetts voted Democratic in all but one presidential election. By 1980, however, Bay Staters seemed ready to make a change. Massachusetts voted for Republican Ronald Reagan in 1980 and 1984, signaling a trend toward more-conservative political views.

Yet, in the mid-1980s, Massachusetts had two liberal Democratic senators: Edward M. Kennedy and John F. Kerry. Until he stepped down in 1986, Congressman Thomas P. "Tip" O'Neill, Speaker of the House, was an eloquent spokesman for arms control and social programs. Other Massachusetts congressmen continue working to protect the environment, improve education, and secure the rights of minorities.

Paradox and contradiction abound in the Bay State's politics. Perhaps the political climate of Massachusetts can best be understood by examining the state's long and fascinating history.

HATHAWAY HIGH

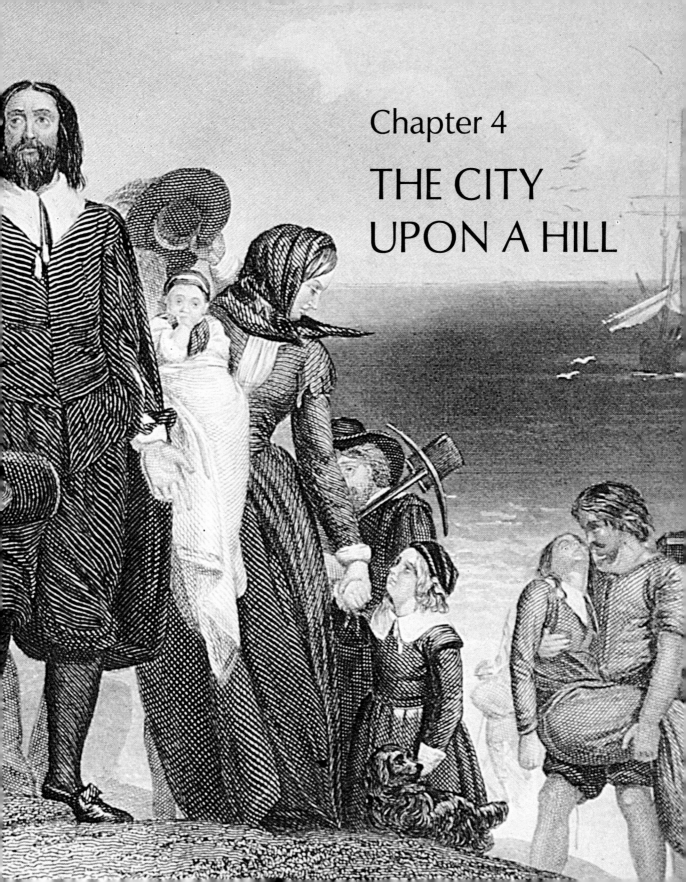

Chapter 4

THE CITY
UPON A HILL

THE CITY UPON A HILL

"We must consider that we shall be a city upon a hill, the eyes of all people upon us." Arriving at the Massachusetts Bay Colony in 1630, John Winthrop exhorted his Puritan followers to the highest spiritual purpose. They would build an ideal community, its members bound together by their deep religious convictions, and they would instruct the watching world by their sublime example.

John Winthrop's vision of an ideal community set the precedent for a series of religious and social movements in the centuries to come. But the history of the land and people of Massachusetts had been unfolding for thousands of years before the Puritans ever set foot in the New World.

THE FIRST PEOPLE OF MASSACHUSETTS

Early in 1986, workers breaking ground for a housing development near the town of Plymouth unearthed a startling array of stone arrowheads and spear points. Within months, scientists realized that they had found the oldest archaeological site ever discovered in Massachusetts.

The people of the Plymouth site belonged to a relatively advanced civilization that arose in Massachusetts around 5000 B.C. They planted corn and squash, made clay pottery, and fished with hooks made of bone. Eventually these people disappeared, apparently driven out by the Algonquian people around 1000 B.C.

The word Algonquian actually refers to a large family of tribes, related by language and customs, who lived throughout the northeastern United States. Several Algonquian groups established themselves within Massachusetts. The Nauset lived on Cape Cod, while the Wampanoag, the Massachusett, and the Patuxet fished and hunted along the coast. The Nipmuck made their home in the central upland, and the Pocumtuc lived in the Connecticut Valley and the Berkshire Hills.

An ancient legend says that a crow came to the Algonquian people from the Great Father in the southwest, bearing a kernel of seed corn in one ear and a bean in the other. Corn and beans were the Algonquians' staple foods. They also raised squash and pumpkins, and gathered wild nuts and berries. The men used bows and stone-tipped arrows to hunt deer, geese, and wild turkeys.

Women played a central role in Algonquian society. They owned the tribe's land, which they cleared and farmed communally. When a young man married, he left home to become a member of his bride's family. Algonquians traced their descent through the families of their mothers and grandmothers rather than through their father's families.

For twenty-five hundred years the Algonquians farmed, hunted, waged war, and made peace with their neighbors. Then, within one short century, their way of life was shattered forever.

EXPLORERS AND TRADERS

As early as A.D. 1000, Viking adventurer Leif Ericson may have landed on Cape Cod. There is even some evidence to suggest that he founded an ill-fated colony there. John Cabot, a Venetian who sailed under the English flag, is believed to have made a visit to Massachusetts in 1498. Sailing south along the coast from Nova Scotia, Cabot claimed all of North America as English territory.

Throughout the 1500s, French and English traders stopped frequently at the coast of Massachusetts. They bargained with the Indians, exchanging beads, rum, and copper kettles for beaver pelts. Unknowingly, they also gave the Indians smallpox, measles, and other European diseases to which the Native Americans had no immunity. By 1617, disastrous epidemics had destroyed as much as two-thirds of Massachusetts' Indian population.

In 1602, British captain Bartholomew Gosnold explored the waters around Cape Cod and built a fort on the island of Cuttyhunk in Buzzards Bay. The fort was soon abandoned, but the British had a growing interest in colonizing the New World. A colony could support itself by farming while sending valuable furs and other goods back to British markets. Besides, America might be just the place for English citizens who were becoming troublesome at home.

PILGRIMS AND PURITANS

On a brisk day in September 1620, an English merchant ship set sail from the port of Southampton with 102 passengers bound for the New World. The ship was called the *Mayflower,* and forty-one of her passengers were Separatists—members of a renegade congregation that had broken away from the Church of England. The Church of England was the only denomination permitted by the British king. But many members felt its doctrines opposed the will of God as expressed in the Bible. Some Separatists were imprisoned for heresy. All lived in fear of persecution. At last a

Before disembarking from the *Mayflower*, William Bradford and the other Pilgrim leaders drafted and signed the Mayflower Compact, a document that became one of the foundation stones of American democracy.

small band arranged to immigrate to America. They thought of themselves as religious pilgrims, undertaking a long and arduous journey in order to worship as they saw fit.

Legend tells us that the Pilgrims first set foot on American soil when they landed at Plymouth Rock. Actually, they anchored for several weeks off the tip of Cape Cod at present-day Provincetown. From there, exploring parties searched the coast for a suitable place to found a village. At last the leaders selected the site at Plymouth, and the *Mayflower* sailed into Plymouth Harbor.

Before the Pilgrims and their fellow passengers disembarked, the group's leaders drafted and signed a document that history recognizes as one of the foundation stones of American democracy. This Mayflower Compact stated that " . . . We whose names are underwritten . . . combine ourselves togeather into a Civill body politick . . . and by vertue thereof to enacte, constitute, and frame such just & equal Lawes, ordinances, Acts, constitutions, & offices . . . as shall be thought most meete & convenient for ye generall good of ye colonie; unto which we promise all due submission and obedience . . . " This marked the first time British colonists saw themselves as a political body with the right to make the laws that would govern them.

Squanto, a Patuxet Indian who spoke English, taught the Pilgrims how to plant corn and fertilize it by burying fish in the soil.

Food was scarce that first winter, and the tiny settlement was ravaged by disease. On March 24, 1621, one colonist wrote in his journal: "Dies Elizabeth, wife of Mr. Edward Winslow. This month thirteen of our number die. And in three months past dies half our company. . . . Of a hundred persons, scarce fifty remain, the living scarce able to bury the dead."

When spring finally came, the Pilgrims found an invaluable friend—a Patuxet Indian named Squanto. A few years earlier, Squanto had been captured by slave traders and sold in Spain. Later he escaped to England, where he became fluent in English. At last he made his way back to his homeland, only to discover that the rest of his tribe had died in the great epidemic of 1617.

Accustomed to English ways, and with no people of his own, Squanto took up residence at the Plymouth colony. He taught the Pilgrims how to plant corn, and how to fertilize it by burying fish in the stony soil. He also served as an interpreter and helped the Pilgrims make an enduring treaty with the Wampanoags and other coastal tribes.

To celebrate their first harvest, the Pilgrims invited the Indians to a three-day feast that later became known as the first Thanksgiving.

To prove their peaceful intentions toward the Indians, the Pilgrims invited them to a great celebration of thanksgiving after their first harvest in October 1621. For three days Pilgrims and Indians feasted together on venison, roast goose, clams, and fish. But, though wild turkeys were plentiful in the surrounding woods, the records make no mention that turkey was on the menu.

Year by year British ships brought more colonists to Massachusetts. Scattered villages arose at Salem, Quincy, Roxbury, and Watertown.

In the spring of 1630, a country squire named John Winthrop landed at Salem with more than a thousand colonists and a raucous supply of goats and chickens. Like the Pilgrims, Winthrop and his followers came to the New World in search of religious freedom. Their beliefs were similar to those of the Separatists, but they had never formally broken with the Church of England. They hoped instead to purify it by working from within. For this reason they were called *Puritans.* The Puritans established the prosperous Massachusetts Bay Colony at the site of present-day Boston. Eventually the Bay Colony absorbed the smaller settlements along the coast to form the British colony of Massachusetts.

LIFE IN COLONIAL MASSACHUSETTS

Humorist H. L. Mencken once defined Puritanism as "the
haunting fear that someone, somewhere, may be happy." Though
Mencken's comment may be too harsh an assessment of the
Puritan outlook, it is true that by today's standards, some aspects
of Puritan life seem severe and joyless. The Puritans saw man's
nature as inherently sinful; one could attain salvation only by
God's grace. Entertainments such as dancing and the theater were
invitations to the devil, and the celebration of Christmas was
condemned as a pagan practice. Yet in government, education,
and many other fields, the Puritans were innovators who made an
enduring contribution to American life.

They also found virtue in hard work. Every man, woman, and
child was expected to work to the best of his or her abilities,
however humble the task. Life was full of hardships, and
everyone had to pitch in if the colony were to survive.

The Puritans felt that the law must be strictly obeyed if the
community were to remain strong. Criminals were punished with
physical penalties that had been part of the English penal system.
A set of wooden stocks stood in the center of many Massachusetts
towns. With arms and legs immobilized, wrongdoers endured
agonies of public humiliation for crimes ranging from swearing to
assault. Ironically, the man who built the stocks in Boston was the
first to occupy them, when it was discovered that he had padded
his bill.

John Winthrop and his followers came to Massachusetts seeking
freedom to practice their own religion. They were not, however,
concerned with the principle of religious freedom, and they had
no tolerance for the beliefs of others. They believed that they
alone possessed the truth. In the 1660s, Puritan authorities hanged

Left: A person who disobeyed the colony's laws might be publicly whipped or placed in the town stocks. Above: Written testimony given by a witness during the Salem witchcraft trials

several Quakers as heretics after they repeatedly returned from exile to preach in Boston.

Like most Europeans of their day, the Puritans were superstitious. Storms, snakes, and illnesses were seen as signs from Satan or warnings from God. Fear and superstition reached their height with the notorious witchcraft trials at Salem Village.

During the long, dreary winter of 1692, nine-year-old Betty Parris and her eleven-year-old cousin Abigail Williams spent their afternoons with Tituba, a West Indian slave woman who worked for Betty's family. Tituba kindled their imaginations with tales of African magic. Soon several older girls joined them for sessions in Tituba's kitchen. When some of the girls began to have strange fainting spells and fits of hysterical crying, they turned on Tituba and accused her of casting a spell over them. Horrified, village officials, led by Betty's father, the Reverend Samuel Parris, demanded to know whether anyone else had been practicing the evil arts. "Yes," the girls chorused. They pointed out an elderly woman whom they all disliked, and the witchhunt began in earnest.

Neighbor began accusing neighbor. A farmer turned a beggar

Harvard College (above) was founded
by the Puritans in 1636.
During King Philip's War (right),
Indians attacked and burned several
Massachusetts towns.

woman away from his door, and later that day his cow fell sick.
The farmer concluded that the beggar was a witch and had put the
cow under a curse. In the end, 19 men and women were executed
as witches. Nearly 150 more people were awaiting trial when
authorities in Boston realized that the situation was wildly out of
hand. They brought the proceedings to a halt and freed the
remaining prisoners, but the bitterness of the trials hung over the
colony for many years to come.

However, the Puritans must not be remembered only for their
intolerance and superstition. From the earliest days of the colony,
they revered education. In order to train their clergymen, they
founded a college at New Towne (later renamed Cambridge) in
1636. A few years later, when John Harvard endowed the school
with his small fortune and his personal library, it was named
Harvard College. Harvard was the first institution of higher
learning established in North America.

Sometimes referred to as the "Apostle to the Indians," a Puritan
preacher named John Eliot devoted his life to working with
Massachusetts' native people. He undertook the enormous task of
translating the entire Bible into one of the Algonquian languages.
Convinced that the Indians must adopt English ways before they
could be converted to Christianity, Eliot founded some thirty

"praying towns" for Christianized Indians throughout the colony. Each town had a schoolhouse, and Indians were encouraged to serve as local officials.

Despite Eliot's efforts, however, the long peace between the settlers and the Indians collapsed in 1675. Year by year, the Europeans had encroached ever deeper into the Indians' territory. At last a Wampanoag chief named Metacom, known to the whites as King Philip, secretly organized several neighboring tribes for a concerted assault against the invaders. Raiding bands of Wampanoags, Pocumtucs, Nipmucks, and Narragansetts from nearby Rhode Island attempted to wipe out the colonists. They burned the frontier towns of Springfield, Hadley, and Northampton, and raided dozens of other settlements. In retaliation, colonial militia attacked Indian villages, sometimes massacring entire populations. Although King Philip was killed in 1676 by an English musketball, raids and skirmishes continued for two more years. King Philip's War finally ended in 1678 with the defeat of the Indians, but not before hundreds of men, women, and children on both sides had been killed.

But no setback could crush the Puritans' determination to tame the wilderness. They built churches, opened shops, and connected their villages with a network of roads. They coaxed crops from the reluctant soil and fished the schools of cod that swarmed the coastal waters. Each town in the Bay Colony held regular town meetings, giving the property-holding men of the community a direct voice in their government. These town meetings, still held in some New England towns today, are an example of democracy in its purest form.

The Puritans were survivors. Undaunted by hardship, they created a thriving colony that would become the intellectual and economic hub of the New World.

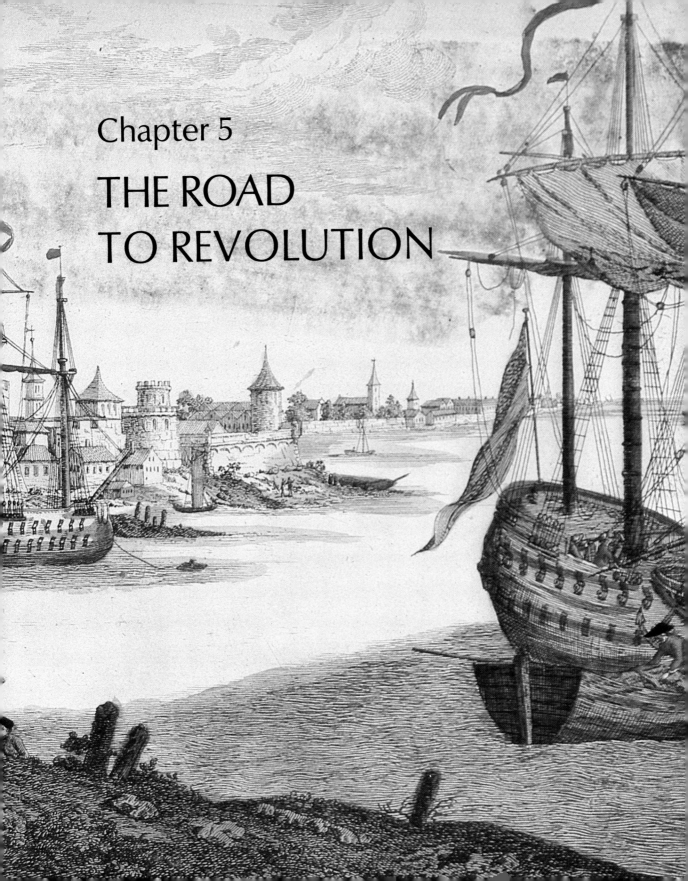

Chapter 5

THE ROAD TO REVOLUTION

THE ROAD TO REVOLUTION

By the early 1700s, Massachusetts was the center of shipbuilding and commerce in the British colonies. Vessels built at Salem, Marblehead, Gloucester, and Boston reached ports all over the world. Foreign goods ranging from fine linens to tea were unloaded on Boston's docks, while American lumber and dried codfish were shipped off to European ports.

The people of Massachusetts were prosperous, well-educated, and accustomed to managing their own affairs. When the British Parliament tried to control them, the colonists smoldered with resentment. One after another, grievances piled up like a heap of dry tinder, ready for the spark that would ignite the fires of revolution.

EMBERS OF DISCONTENT

In 1754, England became embroiled in a long and costly war with France. Known in North America as the French and Indian War and in Europe as the Seven Years' War, the conflict drained England's treasury. Suddenly the mother country saw the colonies as an untapped source of revenue. In 1765 Parliament passed the Stamp Act, one of a series of new taxes to be imposed on the colonies. The Stamp Act required colonists to pay a tax on legal documents, newspapers, and even decks of playing cards. It

When the British Parliament (above left) passed the Stamp Act, colonial leaders such as John Adams (above center) were outraged. In Boston, tax stamps were burned publicly in protest (right).

affected nearly everyone in the colonies on a daily basis. The colonists had no representatives in Parliament. Why, they asked each other, should they submit to Parliament's laws? "No taxation without representation!" became the cry.

At a town meeting in Braintree (now called Quincy), a young lawyer named John Adams delivered a fiery speech. If the colonies bowed to Britain's demands, he declared, they would soon become "the most sordid and forlorn of slaves."

The merchants of Boston led a boycott of British goods, a move soon supported by New York and Philadelphia. The tactic succeeded, and in 1766 Parliament repealed the Stamp Act. The people of Massachusetts celebrated with blazing bonfires. In Boston's West Church, the minister preached on the text "The snare is broken, and we are escaped." But the problems between England and her colonies had only begun.

In 1767, Parliament levied the Townshend Acts, a set of import duties on a wide variety of goods. Once again, Massachusetts led a movement of protest. This time, Britain stationed troops in Boston to restore order.

UnhappyBoston! fee thy Sons deplore,
Thy hallow'd Walks befmear'd with guiltlefs Gore.
While faithlefs P—n and his favage Bands,
With murd'rous Rancour ftretch their bloody Hands;
Like fierce Barbarians grinning o'er their Prey,
Approve the Carnage and enjoy the Day.

If fcalding drops from Rage from Anguifh Wrung
If fpeechlefs Sorrows lab'ring for a Tongue,
Or if a weeping World can ought appeafe
The plaintive Ghofts of Victims fuch as thefe:
The Patriots copious Tears for each are fhed,
A glorious Tribute which embalms the Dead.

But know Fate fummons to that awful Goal,
Where Juftice ftrips the Murd'rer of his Soul;
Should venal C—ts the fcandal of the Land,
Snatch the relentlefs Villain from her Hand,
Keen Execrations on this Plate infcrib'd,
Shall reach a Judge who never can be brib'd.

Engrav'd Printed & Sold by Paul Revere Boston

Crispus Attucks (above) was one of
the colonists killed in the Boston
Massacre (right), depicted here in
an engraving by Paul Revere.

The people of Boston felt as if they were being occupied by an
enemy power. One night in March 1770, the mounting tension
exploded in a skirmish that became known as the Boston
Massacre. A crowd of angry colonists had gathered in the street to
taunt a redcoated British soldier who was guarding the Custom
House. When other troops rushed to his aid, they were pelted
with stones. Enraged, the soldiers fired their muskets into the
unarmed crowd, killing five of the colonists. The first to fall was a
young black man named Crispus Attucks. He is remembered to
this day as the first American to die in the struggle for
independence.

TEA AND TROUBLE

In 1773, yet another law from Parliament stirred the colonists to
a mood of rebellion. The Tea Act placed a duty on the importation
of tea and granted a monopoly on its sale to the British East India
Company. For colonial tea merchants, the act spelled disaster.

In 1773, to protest the Tea Act, fifty colonists dressed as Indians boarded a British East India Company ship and threw chests of tea into Boston Harbor.

When three East India Company tea ships anchored in Boston Harbor, a committee of colonists demanded that the royal governor send them away. But Governor Thomas Hutchinson, a loyal servant of the Crown, refused to comply. On the night of December 16, 1773, fifty colonists dressed themselves as Indians and boarded the ships. Quietly and methodically, they seized the chests of tea and emptied them overboard.

Other than the tea, the only property that was destroyed was one brass padlock, which was later replaced. It was a smooth, orderly demonstration of protest. Yet John Adams saw this "Boston Tea Party" as an indisputable statement of colonial self-determination. "Now the die is cast," he wrote. "The people have crossed the river and cut away the bridge. This is the grandest event which has ever yet happened."

THE SHOT HEARD ROUND THE WORLD

When word of the Boston Tea Party reached London, the British leaders were furious. Parliament passed a series of "Coercive Acts" to punish the rebels. The acts limited the power of the town meetings and stripped the colonists of the right to appoint judges and juries. Worst of all, the British navy blockaded Boston, closing the port to all trade. It was as if England had declared war on Massachusetts.

Within weeks, unemployment soared and supplies of food ran low. Massachusetts' plight awakened a sense of patriotism in the other colonies. Farmers from New York and Pennsylvania donated livestock, wheat, and clothing to beleaguered Boston. One generous contribution came from a Virginia planter named George Washington.

In the summer of 1774, the colonists sent delegates to a Continental Congress that met in Philadelphia. Samuel Adams (the cousin of John Adams) and John Hancock were among those who represented Massachusetts. The congress urged the colonies to prepare for war with Great Britain.

In towns all over Massachusetts, farmers and shopkeepers formed bands of militia and practiced maneuvers on the village greens. They called themselves minutemen, boasting that they could be ready for action at a minute's notice.

In April 1775, British army General Thomas Gage decided it was time to act. He ordered his troops to Lexington, fifteen miles west of Boston, where they were to capture the rebel leaders Adams and Hancock. They were then to march on to Concord and seize a supply of colonial muskets and gunpowder. Alert to every British move, the Boston rebels guessed what was afoot. But someone had to warn the colonial militia that the British were on their way.

In his famous poem "Paul Revere's Ride," Henry Wadsworth Longfellow recounted how Paul Revere set out from Boston and galloped through the night to rouse the minutemen. Actually, Revere was one of three messengers. He reached Lexington in time to warn Adams and Hancock of their peril, but was captured by a British patrol an hour later. His companions, William Dawes and Dr. Samuel Prescott, spread the alarm all the way to Concord.

At 2:00 on the morning of April 19, Captain John Parker assembled his band of sixty minutemen on the Lexington village

On the night of April 19, 1775, Paul Revere rode from Boston to Lexington to warn his fellow patriots that the British were on their way.

green. "Stand your ground," he told them. "Don't fire unless fired upon, but if they mean to have a war, let it begin here." Shortly before dawn, four hundred British soldiers marched upon the village. Seeing themselves hopelessly outnumbered, the minutemen retreated. But the British surrounded them and opened fire. In the ensuing battle, eight colonists were killed and ten were wounded, while the British suffered only one wounded soldier.

The British then headed for Concord, where after another skirmish, they captured some of the military supplies. The Americans, however, were not defeated. As the British marched back to Boston, colonial snipers fired at them from behind trees and stone walls. The bright red coats worn by the British troops made excellent targets for the colonial sharpshooters.

Poet Ralph Waldo Emerson referred to the gunfire exchanged at Concord as "the shot heard round the world" because it marked the beginning of the revolutionary war. Exultant, John Adams proclaimed, "It is a fine day! This is a glorious day for America!"

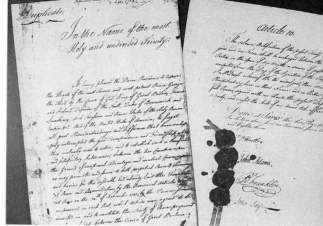

The Battle of Bunker Hill (left) was one of the first major battles of the revolutionary war. John Adams and Benjamin Franklin helped negotiate the peace treaty (right) that ended the war.

THE CHALLENGE OF FREEDOM

Within days of the battle, some ten thousand militiamen from Massachusetts and neighboring colonies surrounded Boston, holding Gage and his troops under siege. On June 17, the British stormed the colonial fortifications on Breed's Hill, just south of Bunker Hill in Charlestown. The Americans were forced to retreat when they ran out of gunpowder, and the English hailed the Battle of Bunker Hill as a victory. But British losses were twice those of the defeated Americans.

Soon after he was appointed commander-in-chief of the Continental army, George Washington decided that the British had to be driven out of Boston. Mounting a formidable set of cannons on Dorchester Heights above the city, he threatened to bombard the British troops. The British were overwhelmed by this show of force. On March 17, 1776, they fled Boston forever. Their departure marked an end to the fighting on Massachusetts soil.

In 1783, the Treaty of Paris granted independence to the thirteen former British colonies. Though the leaders of the revolution had dreamed of liberty for nearly twenty years, independence brought them a fresh set of uncertainties and challenges. "The new government will require a purification of our vices and an augmentation of our virtues," future President John Adams wrote. "The people have unbounded power, and the people are extremely addicted to corruption and venality . . . I must submit all my hopes and fears to an overruling providence."

After the war, Massachusetts staggered under alarming debts. When the governor decided to raise taxes, the farmers of western Massachusetts were outraged. They felt that the officials in Boston were being as distant and uncaring as the British king and his Parliament had been. In 1786-87 a Pelham farmer named Daniel Shays led the men of fifty towns in an armed uprising. At Northampton, Worcester, and Springfield, they shut down the courthouses—symbols of a state government they wanted to reform. About nine hundred state militiamen met Shays and his followers in Springfield. Three of the rebels died under cannonfire and the rest scattered, bringing to an end the uprising's major confrontation. Shays' Rebellion petered out over the succeeding months, and Daniel Shays himself fled the state.

For four years after the close of the war, the former colonists had little sense of themselves as a nation with common needs and goals. When a convention in Philadelphia drafted a federal constitution, many people in Massachusetts were suspicious. They worried that a faraway, centralized government would levy unjust taxes again, and would limit the power of their town meetings. Finally their trusted leaders, Samuel Adams and John Hancock, gave their support to the federal cause. On February 6, 1788, Massachusetts became the sixth state to ratify the United States Constitution.

A century and a half had passed since the Pilgrims and the Puritans set out to found an ideal community in the wilderness. Now their descendants had built a new nation, and its future lay before them, waiting to be discovered.

Chapter 6
CHANGES IN THE OLD ORDER

CHANGES IN THE OLD ORDER

During the nineteenth century, Massachusetts became a leader in the manufacture and export of textiles, leather goods, and a host of other products throughout the country. But ideas were the state's most important export of all. Wherever they went, the people of Massachusetts spread their respect for learning, their love of liberty, and their Puritan dedication to hard work. Across the young American nation, they sowed the seeds of Yankee culture.

TRADE AND EMBARGO

The early years of independence were generous to Massachusetts. Freed at last from duties and restrictions, Boston and other coastal towns imported cane sugar from the Indies, cotton from the southern states, furs from the Pacific Northwest, and woolen cloth from Europe.

In 1807, however, this era of prosperity ended abruptly. England and France were locked in a bitter sea war, and both countries' ships sometimes captured American vessels. Anxious to keep the United States out of the conflict, President Thomas Jefferson passed the Embargo Act, bringing an end to all foreign trade.

In eastern Massachusetts, nearly everyone suffered, from the wealthiest merchant to the humblest dock worker. Newspaper

Some of the sailors involved in Massachusetts' thriving whaling trade (right) passed the time by making carvings called *scrimshaw* out of whalebone or whale teeth (left).

columnists showed their contempt for the new law by spelling it backwards, calling it "Ograbme." One Newburyport poet lamented:

> Our ships all in motion once whitened the ocean,
> They sailed and returned with a cargo.
> Now doomed to decay, they have fallen-a-prey
> To Jefferson—worms—and embargo.

Despite Jefferson's precautions, the United States plunged into war with Britain in 1812. Not until peace was restored in 1815 were Massachusetts' ships free to sail the high seas once more. Some port towns, such as Newburyport and Marblehead, never fully recovered from the embargo. Others, including Salem and Boston, launched a thriving trade with the Orient, importing ivory, carpets, and intricately carved furniture. New Bedford and Nantucket led the nation's whaling trade. Until the 1860s their ships circled the globe, bringing home whale oil to fuel the nation's lamps.

Yet the years of embargo had brought about a major change in Massachusetts' economy. No longer able to depend on foreign trade, the people of Massachusetts had been forced to begin manufacturing goods at home. Never again would the economy depend so heavily upon shipping. The industrious Yankees had discovered some profitable alternatives.

YANKEE INGENUITY

From the earliest days of the Bay Colony, farm families rarely passed an idle hour. During the long winter months when snow blanketed the fields, the men made farm tools and new harnesses for their teams. The women boiled tallow for soap and candles, and spun thread to make the family's clothing. Over the years, some families found it was more profitable to sell the goods they made than to till the stubborn soil.

By the late 1700s, small makeshift factories using water-powered looms to manufacture cotton or woolen fabric sprang up here and there across the state. During the embargo years, many Boston merchants shifted their investment dollars from ships to industry.

In 1810, a Newburyport businessman named Francis Cabot Lowell took his family to Europe for an extended visit. For two years he toured textile mills in England and Scotland, learning everything he could about methods and machinery. He returned to Massachusetts with the dream of opening a factory on a scale never seen before. In one building, he intended to combine all of the processes required to turn raw fiber into finished cloth.

Enlisting the help of his brother-in-law, Patrick Tracy Jackson, Lowell opened his small mill at Waltham on the Charles River in 1815. Some two hundred girls from surrounding farms and villages moved into dormitories and spent their days at spinning wheels and looms. While many smaller mills were shutting down

By 1860, the Bay State had become the nation's leading producer of shoes and textiles. This nineteenth-century drawing shows workers flooding out of a New England factory after a long day of work.

due to English competition, the Waltham factory prospered and grew. Lowell demonstrated that one large operation could work far more cheaply and efficiently than several small ones.

After Lowell died in 1817, Jackson took full control of the business. In 1820, he set out to turn 4 square miles (10.4 square kilometers) of farmland on the Merrimack River into a planned industrial community, complete with schools, churches, and stores. With thirty-five hundred workers by 1828, the city of Lowell served as a model for later "company towns" across the country.

By the 1850s, Massachusetts had become a hive of industry. New textile mills hummed at Lawrence and Fall River. Paper was made in Worcester, firearms were manufactured in Springfield, and boots and shoes were hammered together in Lynn and Brockton. From the Berkshires to Cape Cod, mechanics found work repairing factory equipment and inventing faster, better machines. Other northeastern states followed Massachusetts' lead, gradually turning their energy from agriculture to manufacturing.

Industry brought riches to the factory owners, but the workers themselves struggled for survival. Lowell weavers worked eleven to thirteen hours a day for a modest weekly wage of one to five dollars. Worse yet, most factories employed children as laborers. Nine and ten-year-olds worked the same long hours as their parents and received even lower wages.

As early as the 1830s, workers banded together into unions, striking for higher wages and better working conditions. In some cases, these strikes were successful. In Massachusetts, industry and the union movement rose almost hand in hand.

THE DREAM OF A MORE PERFECT WORLD

While on a tour of Europe in the early 1820s, an idealistic young Bostonian named Samuel Gridley Howe became fascinated by new methods he observed in the education of blind children. When he returned to Boston, he began teaching six blind pupils in his own home. In 1832, he founded the Perkins Institute, the first school for the blind in the United States. Among his students was an eight-year-old girl named Laura Bridgman. Deaf as well as blind, she could not speak and had no way to communicate with the people around her. With patience and ingenuity, Howe taught her to express herself by spelling words with her fingers.

Howe's work with Laura Bridgman illustrated a philosophy that was gaining momentum in Massachusetts—a belief in the untapped potential of every human being. This philosophy stemmed from Unitarianism, a new religious movement that had many followers among Boston and Harvard intellectuals. The Unitarians reacted against the old Puritan concern with man's sinfulness, expressing instead the belief that man's nature is basically good.

Many Unitarians saw this belief in the worth of the individual as a call for social reform. All around them were men, women, and children hopelessly mired in poverty and ignorance. Dorothea Dix launched a national campaign to improve the treatment of people who were mentally ill. Horace Mann crusaded for universal public education. Lucy Stone became a pioneer in

Masthead of *The Liberator*, William Lloyd Garrison's antislavery newspaper

THE LIBERATOR.

OUR COUNTRY IS THE WORLD—OUR COUNTRYMEN ARE ALL MANKIND.

BOSTON, MASS., FRIDAY, JUNE 14, 1850.

the fight for woman suffrage. Although the Unitarians were not prominent in the antislavery movement, their crusading zeal helped to create an atmosphere in which it could develop and flourish among other Protestant sects in Massachusetts.

Though some colonial merchants grew rich by selling slaves in the West Indies, Massachusetts abolished slavery within its borders in 1783. By the early 1800s, most Bay Staters regarded slavery as the greatest evil one human being could inflict upon another. David Walker, a black secondhand-clothes dealer from Boston, became an ardent spokesman for the abolition of slavery. Walker won a small but devoted following among both blacks and whites in Massachusetts, and actually called for a slave revolt in 1829. The movement really gathered force, however, under the leadership of a young journalist from Newburyport named William Lloyd Garrison.

In 1829, Garrison went to work for a newspaper in the slave-holding state of Maryland. Appalled by the conditions he witnessed there, he left to found an antislavery newspaper in Boston called *The Liberator*. Garrison was also a fiery orator. "On this subject I do not wish to think, speak or write with moderation," he proclaimed in a speech near Bunker Hill. "Tell a mother to gradually extract her babe from the fire into which it has fallen, but urge me not to use moderation in a cause like the present! I am in earnest! . . . I will not excuse! I will not retreat one single inch, and I will be heard!"

Many of the thousands of people who left Ireland for America (above) during the Great Potato Famine of the 1840s settled in Massachusetts.

In the decades to come, Garrison's voice *was* heard, along with the voices of Dix, Mann, Stone, and a host of other Massachusetts men and women. Like their Puritan forebears, they dedicated their lives to the goal of shaping a more perfect world.

THE SPREAD OF DIVERSITY

In 1845, the Bunker Hill *Aurora* warned that foreigners were reaching the country at a rate of "13,400 a month, 466 a day, 19 an hour!" Three years later, the same paper shouted, "Our country is literally being overrun with the miserable, vicious and unclean paupers of the old country."

Most of the immigrants who flocked to America's shores in the 1840s were indeed poor and miserable. In their native Ireland, a disease called late blight had destroyed the potato crop. The potato was a staple of the Irish diet, and the blight caused a famine that claimed more than a million lives.

As many as a thousand Irish people a month poured into Massachusetts, desperately hoping to rebuild their lives. They found work in the factories of Boston, Lawrence, Lowell, and Worcester. One of these penniless newcomers took a job at an East Boston barrel factory. His name was Patrick Kennedy.

A great gulf separated the wealthy, educated Brahmins from the struggling Yankee farmers and factory workers. Both classes, however, saw the flood of Irish-Catholic immigrants as a threat to the very foundation of Massachusetts society. Many of the reformers who battled to free black slaves in the South bemoaned the "sea of ignorance, swollen by waves of misery and vice, pouring from . . . Europe upon our shores."

In 1861, however, the Irish question melted into the background. For decades, tension had mounted between the North and South, much of it focused on the issue of slavery. When the Southern states seceded to form a nation of their own, President Abraham Lincoln called for armed troops to help preserve the Union. Massachusetts was the first state to respond, recruiting fifteen hundred eager young soldiers.

Throughout the war, Massachusetts factories supplied guns, uniforms, and boots to the union army. Thousands of young men marched to the battlefields, and several thousand of them never returned.

By the time the war was over, the Irish immigrants of the 1840s and 1850s had begun climbing the social ladder. They founded businesses, saved money, and bought their own homes. Yet they were still scorned by the Yankees and Brahmins, who considered themselves the only "real" Americans. Many employers still posted the notice No Irish Need Apply.

In their quest for power and social standing, the Irish Americans turned their energy to politics. Excluded from the Republican party because of its anti-Irish stance, they became ardent Democrats. They first won seats on city councils, then won them in the General Court (the state legislature). In the 1880s, Hugh O'Brien became Boston's first Irish mayor. In 1892, Patrick Joseph "P.J." Kennedy, son of the East Boston barrel maker, was elected to the state senate. The Irish had become a political force with which to be reckoned.

In the 1880s and 1890s, fresh waves of immigrants poured into Massachusetts—Italians, Jews, Germans, Slavs, Poles, Portuguese, and French Canadians. For the first time in Massachusetts' long history, Yankees found themselves in the minority. Many lamented that their culture was being diluted, drowned in a babble of foreign tongues. In 1896, United States Senator Henry Cabot Lodge, a descendant of two of Boston's most elite families, sponsored a bill to restrict immigration. He presented before Congress a "scientific study" to prove that southern and eastern Europeans were racially inferior, disproportionately poor, diseased, and prone to crime. President Grover Cleveland vetoed the restriction bill in 1896, but it was widely supported in Massachusetts.

Despite these internal conflicts, Massachusetts remained at the forefront of American industry. Mills along the Connecticut River produced one-fourth of the nation's paper. Lawrence and Lowell were major producers of woolen textiles, and Fall River led the nation in cotton manufacturing. Brockton, Lynn, and Haverhill were thriving centers of the shoe industry. In 1900, half of the shoes worn in the United States were made in Massachusetts.

By the turn of the century, Massachusetts was reeling under the social changes of the previous fifty years. Yet the embattled Yankee establishment had to admit one thing about the immigrants who flocked to their cities. Like the Puritan founders, they were ready and willing to throw themselves into hard work, however humble the job might be.

Chapter 7

INTO THE TWENTIETH CENTURY

INTO THE TWENTIETH CENTURY

"Select a few old-fashioned Yankees, full-blooded Americans, to instill a little Americanism in Boston!" So advised one strike breaker when Boston's predominantly Irish police force walked off the job in 1919. His words echoed the sentiments of many Protestant Yankees in Boston and throughout the state.

Well into the twentieth century, Massachusetts was torn by strife between ethnic groups. Through a long series of confrontations, the people of the Bay State struggled painfully for mutual acceptance and racial harmony.

CLASHES AND QUESTIONS

By the 1910s, the political scene in Boston and many other Massachusetts industrial cities was controlled largely by the descendants of Irish immigrants. Even so, the old Brahmin elite still refused to accept the Irish as social equals. Slowly but relentlessly, the Irish fought their way up the ladder of success.

In industry, the Yankee establishment held the reins of power. A series of strikes had won some improvements for factory workers as early as 1874, when women and children were granted a ten-hour workday. But immigrant laborers continued to work long, hard hours for pitiable wages, while factory owners and investors lived in luxury. In 1912, more than twenty-two thousand textile workers staged a massive strike in Lawrence. In

Governor Calvin Coolidge called in the state police to restore order during the 1919 Boston Police Strike.

panic, the city called in the state militia, reinforced with two companies of cavalry. For weeks Lawrence was a city under siege, until strikers and mill owners reached a compromise agreement.

To many Yankees, the movement to form labor unions seemed a threat to the established social order. In 1919, Boston's mayor forbade the police department to join the American Federation of Labor (AFL). In protest, more than a thousand officers walked out on strike. When Republican Governor Calvin Coolidge summoned state police to restore order, he was applauded all across the state, as well as across the nation.

Coolidge's handling of the police strike strengthened his reputation nationwide. In 1920, he became vice-president of the United States under Warren Harding. He was sworn in as president after Harding's death, and was elected to the office in 1924. In his first year as president, Coolidge signed into law Henry Cabot Lodge's long-cherished bill to restrict immigration.

DEPRESSION AND RECOVERY

During World War I, work was plentiful and wages were relatively high. But when the war ended, factory owners began moving their plants to the southern states, where labor was cheaper. Shoe-industry workers nicknamed such plants "factories on wheels." In 1921, Massachusetts slipped into a serious recession. The tireless whirr of machinery fell silent. Equipment rusted in abandoned factory buildings and vast warehouses stood empty, while thousands of men and women searched hopelessly for work.

A century earlier, Massachusetts had led the nation into the age of industry. Now it led the way into the terrible economic depression that engulfed the country in the 1930s. By 1931, only 44 percent of the state's workers were employed full-time.

The state government launched a series of relief programs to assist the unemployed and their families. More help came in 1933, when President Franklin D. Roosevelt's New Deal created thousands of jobs across the country. In Massachusetts, young men built schools, libraries, and roads, and helped to develop recreation areas.

Real recovery did not come, however, until the United States plunged into World War II. Factories reopened to meet the need for weapons, aircraft, and uniforms. Decaying shipyards at Quincy and Lynn came to life. As Massachusetts' men and women flung themselves into the war effort, the state achieved almost full employment—and there were still more jobs to be filled. Thousands of blacks migrated from the southern states to work in the war plants of Boston, Worcester, and other Massachusetts cities.

After the war, the shoe and textile industries sagged once more.

But wartime electronics research had established Harvard University and the Massachusetts Institute of Technology as immense resource centers. When America rushed into the space race in the 1950s, the government turned to the vast scientific expertise of those two remarkable institutions. Generous contracts lured top physicists and engineers to the state. Research laboratories and new "high-tech" industries sprang up along Route 128 west of Boston.

This new appreciation of Harvard and M.I.T. spread to Massachusetts' many other fine colleges and universities. Education became a major industry, bringing in millions of federal dollars. In addition, Boston emerged as a center for banking, insurance, and medicine. New hotels mushroomed along Cape Cod, and ski resorts dotted the slopes of the Berkshires. In the early 1800s Massachusetts' economy had shifted from trade to manufacturing. Now it adapted to changing times by shifting from manufacturing to technology, service, and finance.

THE KENNEDY PHENOMENON

After he graduated from Harvard in 1912, Joseph Kennedy entered the world of banking. When he took over an East Boston bank at the age of twenty-five, he became the youngest bank president in the nation. He moved his family to the Yankee suburb of Brookline, and bought a summer home in Cohasset, a strictly Brahmin resort.

Despite his success, the old-line Bostonians still saw Joe Kennedy as an upstart Irishman who did not know his proper place. When they barred him from joining the Cohasset Country Club, Kennedy founded his own resort at Hyannis on Cape Cod. But he was determined to break the final barriers keeping Irish-

Throughout the twentieth century, the American public has followed the lives of the Kennedys, Massachusetts' most famous family. Clockwise from top left: Joe and his wife Rose in the 1920s; Rose with five of their nine children (Kathleen, Robert, Edward, Patricia, and Jean) on their way to England in 1938; John and his fiancée Jacqueline Bouvier in 1953; Robert and John in the 1950s

American Catholics from obtaining power and prestige. He began grooming his four sons—Joseph Jr., John, Robert, and Edward— for careers in national politics. Joe Jr. was killed during World War II, but the three surviving Kennedy brothers all fulfilled their father's ambitions.

In 1946, the handsome, twenty-seven-year-old war hero John Fitzgerald Kennedy was elected to the United States House of

Representatives. In a race for the Senate six years later, he defeated Henry Cabot Lodge, grandson of the senator who once fought to limit immigration. Then, in the summer of 1960, Kennedy won the Democratic nomination for president of the United States. In the closest presidential election in recent history, Kennedy defeated Republican candidate Richard M. Nixon by only 120,000 popular votes. The great-grandson of a penniless immigrant laborer stepped into the White House.

The youthful new president was a master of style and wit. In his inaugural address he stirred his audience to a fresh commitment, declaring, "Ask not what your country can do for you: ask what you can do for your country."

Kennedy appointed his brother Robert attorney general. In 1962, his youngest brother Edward won a seat in the Senate. Opponents grumbled that the old Irish patronage system was at work, but Kennedy's popularity soared ever higher.

On November 22, 1963, Kennedy and his entourage were visiting Dallas, Texas. As the presidential limousine passed a school textbook warehouse, shots rang out, and Kennedy slumped forward. Two hours later, a shocked nation learned that the leader they had grown to admire and respect was dead. To the mourning nation, John F. Kennedy became a martyr. The Kennedy family had to bear even more grief when in June 1968, Robert, too, was killed by an assassin's bullet.

Today, a major New York airport, a performing arts center in the nation's capital, and a host of parks, schools, and libraries across the nation bear the deceased president's name. Yet in generations to come, President Kennedy will probably be remembered not only for his foreign and domestic policies, but also for the fact that he was the first Irish Catholic to hold the highest office in the land.

TOWARD A BRIGHTER FUTURE

Like the Irish, other minority groups in Massachusetts also carried on a long struggle for economic security and social acceptance. In 1956, Foster Furcolo became the first Italian governor in Massachusetts history. Another trailblazer was Governor Michael S. Dukakis, of Greek descent, first elected in 1972. Humberto S. Medeiros, born in the Portuguese Azores and raised in Fall River, was named Archbishop of Boston in 1970, and was appointed a cardinal in 1973.

Migrating chiefly from the rural South, blacks were the largest ethnic group to move to Massachusetts after World War II. Most settled in and around Boston. But they had little education, and unskilled jobs had grown scarce. The newcomers found themselves at the bottom of the social ladder with little hope for advancement.

In 1966, the people of Massachusetts elected Republican Edward Brooke, a black lawyer from Boston and the state's attorney general, to the United States Senate. Brooke was the first black to win a Senate seat in nearly a century. Yet only the year before, while speaking in Boston, black leader Martin Luther King, Jr. had said: "I would be dishonest to say that Boston is Birmingham, or that Massachusetts is Mississippi. But it would be irresponsible of me to deny the crippling poverty and the injustice that exist in some sections of this community. . . . Boston must become a testing ground for the ideals of freedom. . . . This fight is not for the sake of the Negro alone but rather for the aspirations of America itself. All Americans must take a stand against evil."

In 1967, a fourth-grade teacher named Jonathan Kozol wrote a riveting book called *Death at an Early Age*, which exposed the plight of children in a largely black Boston school. With its

Left: In September 1974, on the second day of court-ordered busing in Boston, school buses containing black students were given a police escort as protection against possible violence by anti-busing demonstrators.
Right: In December, several thousand supporters of the school-desegregation plan gathered for an anti-racism march through the streets of Boston.

outdated textbooks and equipment, and with the contempt its white teachers expressed for their black pupils, the Gibson Elementary School mocked Massachusetts' long history of excellence in education. Many civil-rights activists believed that as long as segregated schools like Gibson existed, education for black children would remain inferior. And without adequate education, blacks could not hope to achieve equality.

In 1974, a federal judge ordered Boston to start busing students in order to integrate its public schools. The decision sparked years of turmoil. In all-white South Boston, black students were greeted with hurled bottles and ugly racial epithets. White mothers in Charlestown formed an anti-busing organization that they christened "Powder-keg," "because we have a short fuse." Black parents were dismayed at having to send their children far from home into unfamiliar and often hostile neighborhoods. The furor subsided only gradually, and some critics argue that Boston's schools reaped more harm than good from the busing order.

Yet despite Boston's troubled public-school system, Massachusetts now offers quality education to a broader range of students than ever before. New recruitment policies are now enabling young men and women from the inner city to attend such outstanding colleges as Williams, Smith, and Mount Holyoke. In 1986, 15 percent of Harvard University's students were black, Hispanic, or Asian, and two-thirds of the student body received financial aid.

The shift toward integrated education is demonstrated powerfully at Cathedral High School, a Catholic school in Boston's South End. From a ceramic mural just inside the main entrance gazes a medley of faces—black and white, Asian, Hispanic, and Native American. The faces are actual portraits of some of Cathedral's students. Explains Cathedral's principal, Sister Patricia Keaveney, "Cultural diversity is seen as a gift. We try to celebrate it."

As the twentieth century nears its close, Massachusetts is learning to value its rich diversity. The doors to education and better employment are opening for people from every racial and ethnic background. Perhaps the ethnic elitism of the past has been supplanted by a new form of prejudice, this time based on education and financial success. Nevertheless, people in Massachusetts today have more opportunities then ever before to achieve their fullest potential.

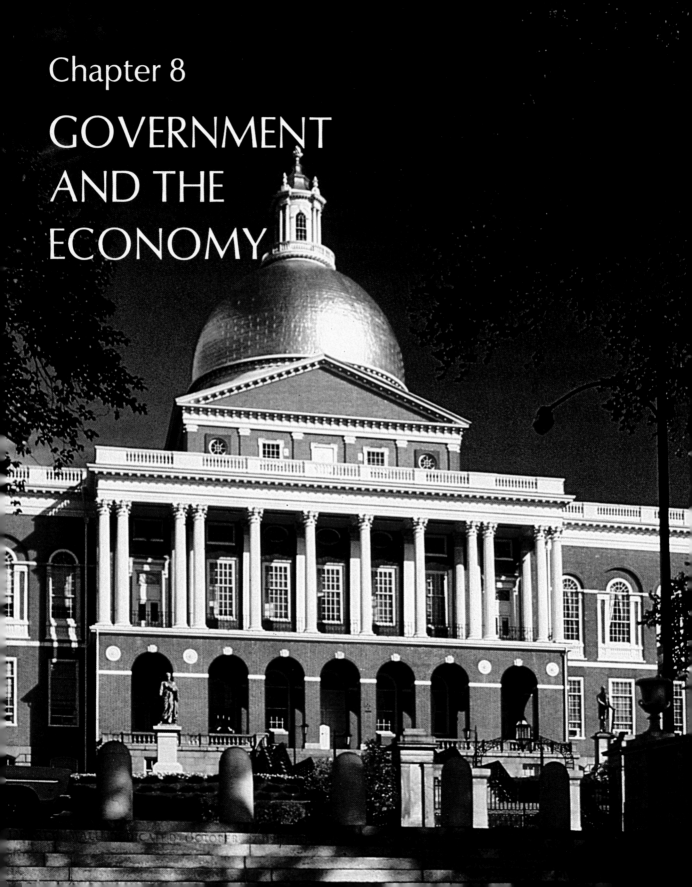

Chapter 8

GOVERNMENT AND THE ECONOMY

GOVERNMENT AND THE ECONOMY

Every year the people of Massachusetts pay billions of dollars in taxes to the state government in Boston. Officials chosen by the people help to decide how these tax dollars shall be used—for schools, libraries, museums, highways, and an array of other vital services. The government and the services it supports are known as the public sector because they are controlled by the public.

The term "private sector" refers to profit-making businesses controlled by individuals or corporations. For Massachusetts to have a healthy economy, public and private sectors must function together smoothly.

STATE GOVERNMENT

On official documents, the Bay State is known as the "Commonwealth of Massachusetts," a title handed down from the state constitution of 1780. This document, which was drawn up by John Adams, preceded the United States Constitution by seven years and is the oldest working constitution in the world.

The government of Massachusetts is divided into three branches. Laws are enacted or repealed by the legislative branch. The judicial branch interprets the laws, and the executive branch, or office of the governor, insures that the laws are carried out.

The state legislature, known officially as the Great and General Court of Massachusetts, consists of a 40-member senate and a

160-member house of representatives. The General Court votes on bills that are proposed by the members themselves or through petitions submitted by qualified voters.

Massachusetts is divided into fourteen counties, each comprising one or more judicial districts. The municipal and district courts are the lowest courts in the state. The superior court, consisting of a chief justice and sixty associate justices, is the state's main trial court. Appeals of civil and criminal cases are referred from the superior court to the appeals court. The highest court in the judicial system is the supreme judicial court in Boston. It consists of a chief justice and six associate justices. Established in 1692, it is the oldest continuously operating court in the nation.

The governor and lieutenant governor of Massachusetts are elected to four-year terms. The governor appoints an eleven-member cabinet to administer various state agencies. The governor also appoints all state judges.

In the 1970s, Massachusetts offered some of the finest health and social services in the country. But during this era, taxes soared until the state earned the nickname "Taxachusetts." In 1980, Massachusetts voters supported Proposition 2½, which radically cut property taxes. Today, about three-fourths of Massachusetts' revenue comes from income, sales, property, and corporate taxes. The remainder is provided through federal programs and grants.

Since colonial days, small towns in Massachusetts have held open town meetings each year in which any registered voter can take part. Larger towns have closed meetings in which only representatives chosen by the voters may participate. During or shortly after a town meeting, selectmen (representatives) are chosen to carry out the voters' wishes until the next meeting.

Massachusetts has a long tradition of excellence in education. In 1647, it became the first American colony to require that public elementary schools (left) be set up in towns with fifty or more households.

EDUCATION

Since the Puritans believed that being able to read the Bible was a necessary step toward salvation, literacy and education were highly valued in Puritan culture. The Boston Latin School opened in 1635, beginning Massachusetts' long tradition of excellence in education. By the 1650s, "common schools" supported by tuition and local taxes sprang up all over the Bay Colony. In 1852, Massachusetts became the first state to require school attendance. Today, all Massachusetts children between the ages of six and fifteen must be enrolled in school.

Some of Massachusetts' outstanding preparatory schools (private schools that ready students for college) have earned national reputations. Such "prep" schools as Phillip's Andover Academy, Groton, Northfield-Mount Hermon, and Deerfield uphold a long tradition of quality private education.

With about 120 colleges and universities, Massachusetts is a haven for students. Five outstanding schools cluster together in the Connecticut Valley: The University of Massachusetts, Hampshire College, and Amherst College in Amherst; Smith College in Northampton; and Mount Holyoke College in South

Hadley. Founded in 1837 by a teacher named Mary Lyon, Mount Holyoke was the first women's college in the United States. The city of Worcester has ten colleges and universities, including Clark University and College of the Holy Cross.

The Boston area, with more than twenty colleges and universities, is one of the world's great education centers. Highly regarded schools include Tufts University in Medford, Brandeis University in Waltham, and Wellesley College in Wellesley. Boston's Northeastern University is the largest private university in the country. Other leading schools in Boston are Boston University, Boston College, and Simmons College. Some of the finest young musicians in the nation are drawn to the Boston Conservatory and the New England Conservatory of Music.

Just west of Boston across the Charles River lies the city of Cambridge, which surrounds Harvard University. Founded in 1636 as a training center for clergymen and magistrates, Harvard is the oldest, most prestigious, and one of the finest universities in America. Among its distinguished graduates are six United States presidents and twenty-nine Nobel Prizewinners. Harvard's graduate programs in law, medicine, government, and business administration have produced some of the nation's leading professionals. With more than nine million volumes, Harvard has the largest university library in the world.

In 1986 Harvard celebrated its 350th birthday. An exuberant parade featured tumblers, clowns, and stiltwalkers. A six-hundred-foot helium-filled plastic rainbow arched across the Charles River, while a vast light show depicted the thirty-foot hand of John Hancock (class of 1754) signing the Declaration of Independence. Many grumbled that the gaudy festivities were out of place at such a dignified institution. But even the critics admitted that Harvard had plenty to shout about.

Among Massachusetts' many institutions of higher learning are Harvard University (left), M.I.T., (below), and the University of Massachusetts at Amherst (bottom left). Students and visitors alike enjoy strolling through bustling Harvard Square, which is loaded with interesting shops and restaurants (bottom right).

Boston, New England's main seaport (right), handles about 20 million tons of cargo a year. Fall River is the state's second-most important port.

Cambridge is also home to the Massachusetts Institute of Technology (M.I.T.), established in 1861. Preeminent as a center of scientific training and research, it offers some of the finest programs in engineering, social and physical sciences, management, and architecture. Today it is best known for its leadership in the computer revolution. The computer center at M.I.T. is open twenty-four hours a day, and it is busy even on Saturday nights.

TRANSPORTATION AND COMMUNICATION

Boston's Logan International Airport is the busiest airport in Massachusetts and the hub of air travel in New England. In addition, Massachusetts has 25 other public airports and 135 private fields. Boston is the state's chief seaport, followed by Fall River.

Massachusetts has 33,800 miles (54,400 kilometers) of highways and paved roads. The state's only toll road is the Massachusetts Turnpike (commonly known as the Mass Pike), which stretches from Boston to the New York state line. About 1,650 miles (2,660 kilometers) of railroad tracks crisscross Massachusetts, carrying freight and passengers from all over the country. Begun in 1897, Boston's subway system is the oldest in the United States.

In 1690, Boston published the first newspaper in the British colonies, *Publick Occurrences Both Forreign and Domestick*. Today some 240 newspapers are printed in Massachusetts, 50 of them dailies. Boston has two daily newspapers: the *Boston Globe*, and the *Boston Herald*. The *Christian Science Monitor*, also published in Boston, has a national circulation and has won many awards for journalistic excellence. Other leading papers in the state include the *Worcester Telegram and Gazette*, the *Springfield Union*, the *Springfield Daily News*, and the *Berkshire Eagle* of Pittsfield.

Massachusetts is the home of more than twenty-five publishing companies. Chief among them are Little, Brown, and Company and Houghton Mifflin in Boston, and Harvard University Press in Cambridge. The Boston-based magazine *Atlantic Monthly* has remained one of the most respected magazines in America since its founding in 1857.

Massachusetts' first radio station, WGI of Medford, began transmitting in 1920. The state's first television stations, WBZ-TV and WNAC-TV, both began operating in Boston in 1948. Many of the fine programs aired on public television channels throughout the country originate at Boston's WGBH-TV. Massachusetts has 13 television stations and approximately 170 radio stations.

INDUSTRY AND TECHNOLOGY

In the nineteenth century, inventors all over Massachusetts developed machines that would make factories run more efficiently. Massachusetts is still a leading producer of equipment used in the textile, printing, and paper industries. Bay State plants also turn out scientific instruments and electrical appliances including lamps, radios, and television sets.

Massachusetts is a leader in the production of highly sophisticated electronic equipment ranging from home computers to aerospace guidance systems. Many of the state's research-and-development facilities are concentrated near Route 128 and Route

495, which arc around Boston. Among the high-tech companies with headquarters in the state are Raytheon Company of Lexington, Digital Equipment Corporation of Maynard, Wang Laboratories of Lowell, and Data General Corporation of Westboro. Massachusetts is one of the top-ranking states in the number of military contracts it receives each year.

Factories in Boston make fabricated metal products such as pipes, heating ducts, and aluminum window frames. Chemical products, processed foods, and paper are also important. Textile mills and clothing factories still operate in towns along the coast. Altogether, manufacturing accounts for 25 percent of Massachusetts' gross state product (GSP), the total value of goods and services produced in Massachusetts in the course of a year.

THE SERVICE ECONOMY

Services, comprising 71 percent of the GSP, are the mainstay of Massachusetts' economy. Service industries are businesses that render services rather than manufacture saleable goods.

With more than one hundred banks and a major stock exchange, Boston is New England's financial center. Boston and Springfield are both important centers of the insurance industry.

Massachusetts' colleges and universities, which employ thousands of people from maintenance workers to professors, contribute significantly to the state's economy. The state also has earned world renown for its outstanding medical facilities. With 248 doctors for every 100,000 people, the Bay State has one of the highest physician-to-patient ratios in the nation. Many top-ranking hospitals are clustered in Boston, including Massachusetts General, Tufts-New England Medical Center, and Brigham and Women's Hospital.

About 13 percent of the state's land is devoted to farming (left). Massachusetts cranberry bogs (above) produce half of the nation's cranberries.

HARVESTING LAND AND SEA

Although only 1 percent of the GSP in Massachusetts comes from agriculture, 13 percent of the state's land is devoted to farming. Most farms are in the western half of the state, but Plymouth and Bristol counties in the south are also agricultural regions.

Greenhouses that raise flowers and ornamental shrubs are the Bay State's leading source of agricultural income. Dairy farming is the state's second-most-important agricultural activity. Massachusetts produces half of the cranberries consumed in the United States. Most of the state's cranberries are grown in Plymouth County. Truck farms produce a variety of vegetables, including asparagus, cucumbers, tomatoes, and corn. Apples and cigar tobacco grow in the fertile Connecticut Valley. The state also produces beef cattle, poultry, and hogs.

Massachusetts is one of the leaders of the nation's fishing industry. The state's largest fishing fleet anchors at New Bedford, where half the annual American scallop catch is hauled in.

Massachusetts is a leading commercial fishing state. New Bedford, Boston, and Gloucester are its three main fishing ports.

Gloucester fishermen bring in shrimp, flounder, and ocean perch. The cod, that staple of the colonial economy, is still fished all along the Massachusetts coast, especially on Cape Cod.

By the late 1950s, Massachusetts' fishing industry began to decline, due to foreign competition and overharvesting in the north Atlantic. In 1977 fishermen rejoiced when an international agreement gave them exclusive rights to fish within 200 miles (322 kilometers) of the United States shore—a vast extension of the previous 12-mile (19-kilometer) limit. But at the same time, the government placed severe restrictions on the number of cod, haddock and yellow-tailed flounder allowed to be taken. Though environmentalists applauded these measures, the fishermen were outraged. "Quotas? It's crazy!" exclaimed one captain to a reporter. "I got no time to fight the quotas. I got to make some money."

As the schools of fish in the North Atlantic gradually replenished themselves, the quotas eased. With careful management by both the government and business interests, Massachusetts' fishing industry should continue to prosper in the years to come.

Chapter 9
ARTS AND LEISURE

ARTS AND LEISURE

Since colonial times, Massachusetts has enjoyed a remarkable heritage in literature and the arts. Boston is sometimes called the ''Athens of America'' after the splendid Greek city that reached a zenith of culture during ancient times.

The people of Massachusetts also know how to relax and have fun. They flock to hear light music as well as the classics, and cheer lustily for their favorite sports teams. Like a richly varied tapestry, the Bay State's culture weaves together all the struggles and pleasures of its diverse people.

LITERATURE

During the 1600s, the Puritans controlled the printed word in Massachusetts. The first English-language book to appear in America was the *Bay Psalm Book*, published in Cambridge in 1640. The book was a collection of Biblical Psalms translated from the Hebrew by some of the colony's most prominent clergymen.

One of the first writers to offer a glimpse into everyday colonial life was Anne Bradstreet, wife of a magistrate and the mother of eight children. She arrived in Massachusetts in 1630 at the age of eighteen and struggled to make a home in the wilderness for her growing family. Somehow she found time to write poetry, much of which was not published until after her death. One of her most moving poems expresses her grief when her house in Andover burned to the ground in 1666:

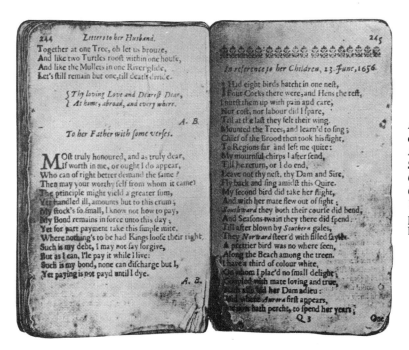

A page from an original copy of Anne Bradstreet's *Several Poems Compiled with Great Variety of Wit and Learning,* published in Boston in 1678

Here stood that trunk, and there that chest,
There lay that store I counted best,
My pleasant things in ashes lie
And them behold no more shall I.

One of the most prolific writers of the colonial era was Cotton Mather. A noted clergyman and the son and grandson of eminent Puritan preachers, Mather once described his life as "a continual conversation with God." Mather published more than four hundred books, many of them collections of sermons and treatises on religion. His most famous work, *Magnalia Christi Americana,* is a history of religious practice in the colonies. He also had a keen interest in the sciences, and a number of his works deal with medicine and natural history. He presented many advanced ideas for his times in *Bonifacius, Or, Essays to Do Good.* In this work Mather recommended reward as a more effective teaching method than punishment, and suggested that a person's mental state might affect his physical well-being.

During his youth in Boston, Benjamin Franklin (left) apprenticed at his brother's printing shop. Longtime Cambridge resident Henry Wadsworth Longfellow (right) was the most popular American poet of his time.

By the early 1700s, some writers had begun to challenge the Puritan establishment. In 1721, James Franklin of Boston founded a lively newspaper, the *New-England Courant*. One morning a satirical column signed "Silence Dogood" appeared under the door of the newspaper office. The "Silence Dogood Papers," which lampooned the pettiness of Boston society, were the secret work of James' seventeen-year-old brother Benjamin. Benjamin Franklin soon left Boston for Philadelphia, where he developed his talents as a writer, inventor, and diplomat.

One of America's best-loved poets is Henry Wadsworth Longfellow. Born in 1807 in Portland, Maine (then part of Massachusetts), Longfellow began teaching at Harvard in 1836 and lived the rest of his life in Cambridge. Many of his works dramatize historic espisodes. Though he sometimes bent facts to suit his artistic purposes, his narrative poems, such as *Evangeline*, *The Song of Hiawatha*, and *The Courtship of Miles Standish*, are still popular today.

In the 1840s, the philosophical movement known as transcendentalism reached its peak. Led by the brilliant poet and essayist Ralph Waldo Emerson, the transcendentalists condemned the narrowness and conformity they saw in conventional society.

In his classic book *Walden*, Henry David Thoreau (above) recounted the experience of living alone for two years in an isolated cabin near Walden Pond (left).

They argued that each individual must follow his own conscience, regardless of civil or religious law, and must avoid yielding blindly to authority. At the close of his essay "Self-Reliance," Emerson wrote, "Nothing can bring you peace but yourself. Nothing can bring you peace but the triumph of your principles."

One of Emerson's followers, Henry David Thoreau, put his transcendentalist ideas into practice by retreating from society and refusing to vote, attend church, or pay taxes. Alarmed by the rise of industry in so many Massachusetts towns, Thoreau left his Concord home in 1845 and moved to an isolated cabin near Walden Pond. For two years he lived in the woods, observing the plants and animals around him and pondering the world he had left behind. While watching a fierce battle between two armies of ants, he reflected on the pointlessness of human warfare. Thoreau recounted his experiences in *Walden*, which appeared in 1854 and remains a literary classic.

Nathaniel Hawthorne was a friend of many of the transcendentalists and was influenced by them, though he did not accept all of their beliefs. From his home in Concord he wrote his greatest novels, *The House of the Seven Gables* and *The Scarlet Letter*. Both are set against the harsh landscape of Puritanism in the Bay

Colony, and depict the cruelty that can be enacted in the name of righteousness.

The writers in the Boston area formed a loose-knit literary community, criticizing and encouraging each other's work. In the town of Amherst, however, one of America's most remarkable poets worked almost entirely alone. Emily Dickinson spent nearly all of her life in her family home, withdrawing deeper and deeper into seclusion with the passing years. Although only seven of her poems were published during her lifetime, after her death, boxes brimming with her verses were rescued for posterity by her sister.

With wit and tenderness, Dickinson wrote about love, nature, and God. She was a master of the precise turn of phrase that could sum up a complex idea or emotion. In one poem about the deaths of her parents, she concludes ironically, "Parting is all we know of heaven, And all we need of hell."

Through the 1890s and into the twentieth century, Massachusetts remained a center for literary achievement. Henry James contrasted American innocence with the worldliness of Europe in such novels as *The Ambassadors* and *The Portrait of a Lady*. His brother William probed the meaning of spirituality in *The Varieties of Religious Experience*. John P. Marquand described Boston's changing way of life in such novels as *The Late George Apley*. Amy Lowell experimented with free verse in her collection of poems called *Sword Blades and Poppy Seeds*.

The threat of nuclear war and the frantic pace of modern life shaped the work of many Massachusetts writers after World War II. For Pulitzer Prizewinning poet Robert Lowell, mental illness came to stand for the ills he saw in society. This symbol is also used by poets Anne Sexton and Sylvia Plath. Their work is highly personal, but all of these poets expose the flaws of society, searching through despair for the path to a better world.

ART

In the early 1700s, portrait painting in Massachusetts was practiced by traveling artists who went from house to house with bundles of partially completed pictures. When they found a customer, they simply painted in his face.

The finest portrait painter of the Bay Colony was John Singleton Copley, born in Boston in 1738. Most painters of his time created idealized portraits, smoothing over their subjects' blemishes and irregular features. Copley, however, depicted vivid, true-to-life personalities. In 1774 he moved to England to study under some of the British masters and remained there for the rest of his life. In Europe his work became more polished, but it lost much of its uniqueness and charm.

In the nineteenth century, two more Massachusetts painters carried on the tradition of becoming expatriates. James Abbott McNeill Whistler was born in Lowell in 1834, but immigrated to Europe in 1855. His best-known painting is *Arrangement in Gray and Black No. 1: Portrait of the Artist's Mother*, better known as simply *Whistler's Mother*. Winslow Homer was born in Boston in 1836. A visit in 1881 to the English fishing village of Tynemouth inspired him to concentrate on painting seascapes and fishermen. When he returned to America, he settled on the coast of Maine, where he continued to paint subjects related to the sea.

Daniel Chester French is one of America's most popular sculptors. Many of his bronze statues were inspired by historical figures or events. French's *The Minute Man*, which stands near the Concord River in Concord, was reproduced on posters and defense bonds during World War II as a symbol of American patriotism. In 1919, French completed his most famous work, a huge, seated statue of Abraham Lincoln commissioned for the

Bay Staters have made important contributions to American art and architecture. Clockwise from top left: John Singleton Copley's portrait of Paul Revere; James McNeill Whistler's *Whistler's Mother*; H. H. Richardson's Trinity Church; Daniel Chester French's *The Minute Man*

Lincoln Memorial in Washington, D.C. *Death Staying the Hand of the Sculptor*, a bronze relief at Forest Hills Cemetery in Boston, is considered by critics to be his most important work.

Early in the twentieth century, the beauty of the Massachusetts coast began to attract artists from all over the country. Today artists' colonies flourish on Cape Ann, Cape Cod, and Martha's Vineyard. Sculptor Walker Hancock left St. Louis for Massachusetts in 1920, and continued to work there for more than fifty years. "I was immediately captivated by the ruggedness of the coast," Hancock explained in an interview. "I knew this was where I wanted to live." Working from his studio in Rockport, Hancock became one of the nation's leading sculptors in marble and bronze.

ARCHITECTURE

Charles Bulfinch was the first true professional architect to work in Massachusetts. Born to a wealthy Boston family in 1763, he studied in Europe, but returned to make his name in New England. Some of his elegant mansions, with their delicate balustrades and slender columns, still stand along Boston's Beacon Street. The great dome of Bulfinch's "new" State House, built in 1795, gleams above the Boston Common.

In 1872, an unknown young architect from New Orleans named Henry H. Richardson won a national competition with his unusual design for a new church to be built on Boston's Copley Square. The building was a massive structure with a surface of rough, colored stone. Richardson's Trinity Church, built in a style sometimes dubbed "Richardson Romanesque," is still considered one of Boston's architectural masterpieces. Richardson left his mark on Massachusetts with a number of other fine buildings,

Two of Boston's most striking modern buildings are City Hall (above), built in 1969 as part of the city's new Government Center; and the gleaming, 60-story John Hancock Tower (right), New England's tallest building.

including the Brattle Square Church in Boston, Sever and Austin halls at Harvard University in Cambridge, and the Crane Memorial Library in Quincy.

In the 1960s, Boston sought out innovative architects once more. As part of a campaign to revitalize the city, Mayor John F. Collins commissioned a magnificent new Government Center. Noted architect I. M. Pei drew the master plan for the sixty-acre (twenty-four-hectare) complex. Its thirty-nine buildings, including the double towers of the John F. Kennedy Federal Office Building, were designed by individual architectural firms. Two broad thoroughfares lead to the nine-story City Hall, which critic Ada Louise Huxtable described as "a tough and complex building for a tough and complex age, a structure of dignity, humanism and power."

MUSIC

Founded in 1881, the Boston Symphony Orchestra has been led by some of the world's most famous conductors, including Serge Koussevitzky, Charles Munch, and Erich Leinsdorf. In 1973, the symphony came under the baton of Japanese-born Seiji Ozawa. The orchestra is based at Boston's Symphony Hall, which is also home to the Boston Pops Orchestra. Boston also has a world-acclaimed ballet troupe, the Boston Ballet. The Boston Opera Company is conducted by Sarah Caldwell, the first woman to conduct a major orchestra.

Outdoor performances by the Boston Symphony are among the highlights of the Tanglewood Music Festival, held every summer in Lenox in Berkshire County. Tanglewood also hosts dozens of popular performers, including folk, rock, and jazz ensembles. Another summer treat is the series of outdoor concerts performed by the Boston Pops on Boston's Esplanade along the Charles River. The Pops charms its audiences with orchestral renditions of songs by Irving Berlin, Rogers and Hammerstein, and even the Beatles. For almost fifty years, the Pops was led by colorful conductor Arthur Fiedler. After Fiedler died in 1979, John Williams became the Pops' conductor.

The Boston Marathon is America's oldest annual long-distance race.

SPORTS

Massachusetts residents enjoy skiing in the Berkshire Hills, swimming and boating off the Atlantic shore, and fishing in the state's many rivers. Track and field events have long been popular. The Boston Marathon, first held in 1897, is America's oldest annual long-distance race. Every year, thousands of runners come from all over the world to participate in this world-famous event. Basketball was invented in Massachusetts in 1891, when teacher James A. Naismith of the Springfield Y.M.C.A. sought to create a new game that could be played indoors during winter months.

Professional sports in Massachusetts are centered in the Boston area. The American-League Boston Red Sox baseball team won pennants as recently as 1986, 1975, and 1967, but one must go back to 1918 for the team's last World Series victory. Through the years, however, the Red Sox have fielded a parade of superstars, including Ted Williams in the 1940s and 1950s, Carl Yastrzemski in the 1960s and 1970s, and Jim Rice in the 1970s and 1980s.

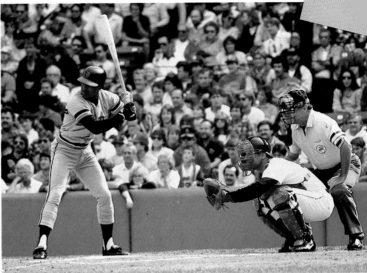

The Boston Celtics play their home games on Boston Garden's famous parquet floor (left). The Boston Red Sox (above) play at Fenway Park, one of America's best-loved ballparks.

Boston's National Hockey League team, the Bruins, have won only two Stanley Cup championships since World War II. During the 1970s, however, the team's great defenseman Bobby Orr dazzled opponents with his skill on skates. The National Football League New England Patriots play their home games at Sullivan Stadium in Foxboro. In 1986 they won a Super Bowl berth, only to be overpowered by the Chicago Bears.

The greatest of all Boston-area franchises is the Boston Celtics basketball team. Between 1946 and 1986, the Celtics won an amazing sixteen NBA championships. Red Auerbach, their general manager and one-time coach, seems to have a golden touch when choosing players. Over the decades he has developed Bob Cousy, Bill Russell, John Havlicek, K.C. Jones (who later became coach of the team), Dave Cowens, Kevin McHale, and Larry Bird. Many experts consider the hard-driving, sharp-shooting Bird to be the most complete player ever to step onto a basketball court.

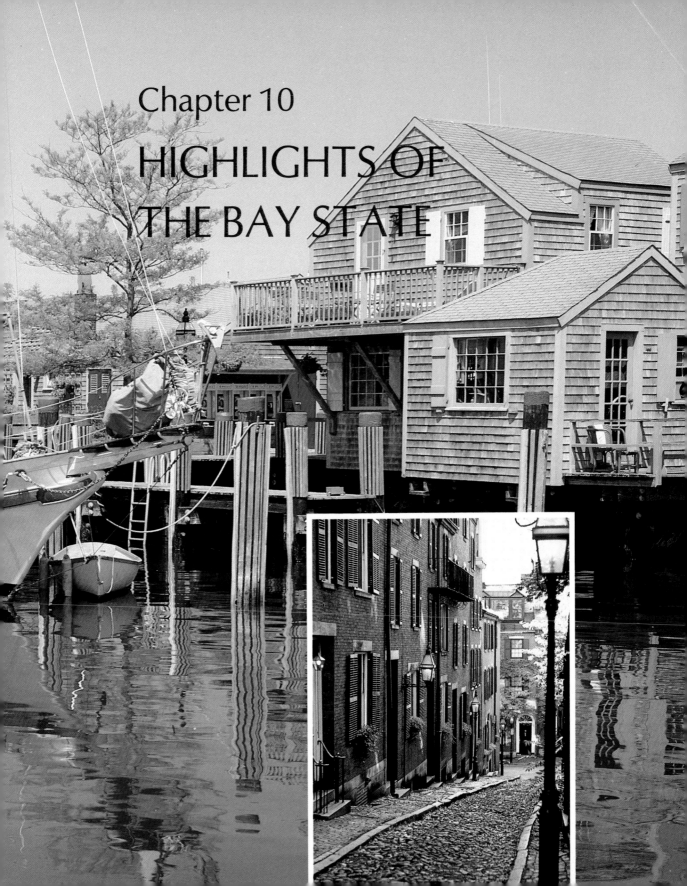

Chapter 10
HIGHLIGHTS OF THE BAY STATE

HIGHLIGHTS OF THE BAY STATE

Though it is one of the smallest states in the Union, Massachusetts offers a broad spectrum of landscapes and life-styles. From the Berkshires to Cape Cod, the visitor can explore hills and quiet villages, bustling cities and sparkling beaches. All along the way are vivid reminders of the state's long and fascinating history, as past and present interweave to form today's Massachusetts.

THE BERKSHIRE HILLS

Though Massachusetts has long been one of America's most heavily industrialized states, the Berkshire Hills in the western part of the state have a unique rural charm. Here 150-year-old covered bridges span bubbling streams, and rough stone walls divide farmers' fields as they did centuries ago. Towns such as Florida, Peru, and Williamstown, with their simple stone churches and picture-book village squares, seem forgotten by time.

The Berkshires offer fresh delights with the changing seasons. In early spring, rural families harvest buckets of sap from wild sugar maples, boiling it down into golden-brown maple syrup. In the summer, the hills come alive with music, drama, and dance festivals. Each year thousands flock to the Tanglewood Music Festival at Lenox and the Jacob's Pillow Dance Festival at Lee. Some of the finest summer theater in the country can be seen at

A look-out point along the Mohawk Trail in western Massachusetts

the Williamstown Theater Festival and the Berkshire Theater Festival in Stockbridge. In the fall, the old Mohawk Trail (a section of Route 2 between Greenfield and Williamstown) and other country roads offer a dazzling spectacle of autumn foliage. In winter, the snow-clad countryside lures eager downhill and cross-country skiers.

CENTRAL MASSACHUSETTS

East of the Berkshires, in the fertile valley of the Connecticut River, prosperous farms grow tobacco, onions, potatoes, and field crops. To meet their cultural needs, the people of the Connecticut Valley draw upon the rich resources of such fine schools as Smith College in Northampton and the University of Massachusetts in Amherst. The Smith College Museum of Art has an outstanding collection of works by Impressionist and modern masters, including Degas, Manet, Renoir, and Picasso. The University Gallery in Amherst, which opened in 1975, offers changing exhibitions by contemporary painters and sculptors.

In the nineteenth century, the waterpower provided by the Connecticut River gave rise to some of Massachusetts' leading industrial cities, including Chicopee, Holyoke, and Springfield. Today Springfield, the third-largest city in the state, is an industrial center that produces chemicals, clothing, machinery, and other goods.

Every fall, visitors flock to western and central Massachusetts to see the spectacular autumn foilage.

The city has several important historic and cultural landmarks. The Springfield Armory, the first United States arsenal, began storing firearms during the revolutionary war and began manufacturing guns in 1795. The armory continued, with few interruptions, to turn out weapons until 1968. The museum at the Springfield Armory National Historic Site displays many weapons that were first developed here, including the Springfield rifle and the M1. The game of basketball originated in Springfield in 1891, and basketball's proudest moments are commemorated in the Naismith Memorial Basketball Hall of Fame. Concentrated around a grassy courtyard know as the Quadrangle are the Connecticut Valley Historical Museum, the Museum of Science, the Springfield Museum of Fine Arts, and the George Walter Vincent Smith Art Museum.

Along the shores of the Quabbin Reservoir in Massachusetts' central uplands, more than 10,000 acres (4,047 hectares) of land have been set aside for recreation and conservation. Hiking trails wind through the woods past such tiny villages as Wendell,

A worker at the Old Sturbridge Village Cooper Shop demonstrates how wooden casks were made in the early 1800s.

Irving, Warwick, and Royalston. The reservoir itself is open to the public for fishing and boating.

Engraved upon the municipal seal of the city of Worcester are the proud words "Heart of the Commonwealth." Worcester (pronounced "wooster"), which lies in the low hills of central Massachusetts some 40 miles (64 kilometers) west of Boston, was a major industrial town by the mid-nineteenth century. Although it is still a leading manufacturing center and is today the Bay State's second-largest city, changes in the economy have shut down many of its once-busy factories. In an effort to revitalize its downtown area, in 1971 the city opened Worcester Center, a glistening complex of office buildings, restaurants, and shops. Worcester is home to Clark University, College of the Holy Cross, the Worcester Polytechnic Institute, and seven other colleges and universities. The Worcester-based American Antiquarian Society boasts the world's largest collection of early-American newspapers, sheet music, children's books, and other printed matter.

Southwest of Worcester is Old Sturbridge Village, a painstaking recreation of an 1840s New England town. A working farm and forty period buildings, including houses, churches, shops, and mills, dot the two-hundred-acre (eighty-one-hectare) grounds. Costumed employees demonstrate how soap, bread, shoes, tinware, and even horseshoes were made long ago.

Saugus Iron Works National
Historic Site outside Boston
is a reconstruction of
America's first ironworks.

GREATER BOSTON

The town of Concord outside Boston was once home to some of
Massachusetts' leading literary figures. On Lexington Road stands
Orchard House, the home of Louisa May Alcott and the setting for
her novel *Little Women*. The homes of Ralph Waldo Emerson and
Nathaniel Hawthorne are also open to the public. Henry David
Thoreau would be aghast, no doubt, if he knew that nearby
Walden Pond, his retreat from the bustle of the world, is now a
popular picnic ground.

Today's Concord lies amid a tangle of highways and suburban
shopping malls. Yet along the Concord River, a famous
monument reminds passersby of a momentous episode in history.
The Minute Man by Daniel Chester French stands near a replica of
the North Bridge, where attacking British Redcoats were met by
minutemen in the opening engagement of the revolutionary war.
Inscribed at the statue's base is the first stanza of Ralph Waldo
Emerson's "The Concord Hymn":

> By the rude bridge that arched the flood,
> Their flag to April's breeze unfurled,
> Here once the embattled farmer stood,
> And fired the shot heard round the world.

The coastline at Marblehead on Massachusetts' North Shore

The northern arm of Massachusetts Bay, commonly known as the North Shore, stretches from Cape Ann south to Boston. Traditionally, the North Shore has been regarded as the "fashionable" side of the bay. The town of Marblehead embodies this image with its Federal-period houses, sumptuous Victorian mansions, and elegant shops. During the summer months, more than eighteen hundred sporting yachts crowd into its tiny harbor.

But many people along the North Shore still earn their livelihood from the sea. From the docks at Gloucester Harbor, a visitor can breathe in the smell of tar and salt air (and, depending on the wind's direction, the reek of cod from the fish-packing plants) while watching the boats come in with the day's catch. Despite weather forecasts and motorized boats, fishing can be a dangerous trade. Every year on a Sunday in August, the people of Gloucester gather for the Fishermen's Memorial Service. Grieving friends and relatives scatter flowers upon the waves while the names of those who perished in the past year are read aloud.

Farther south along the coast, the Charles River empties into Massachusetts Bay. Nestled in the curve of the river's west bank lies the state's fifth-largest city, Cambridge, home of M.I.T. and Harvard University. The heart of the Harvard campus is Harvard Square, a melee of hurrying students, tweed-coated professors, and, occasionally, sign-toting political demonstrators. Harvard's Fogg Art Museum has one of the most extensive university art collections in the world. The Harvard University museums on Oxford Street incorporate museums of zoology, botany, and mineralogy under one roof. The university's Peabody Museum of Archaeology and Ethnology has excellent displays of South American artifacts.

The streets of Cambridge are steeped in history. The Henry Wadsworth Longfellow House, which served as George Washington's headquarters early in the revolutionary war and later became Longfellow's beloved home, is now a national historic site. Mount Auburn Cemetery is the final resting place of some of Massachusetts' most famous sons and daughters, including Longfellow, Charles Bulfinch, Mary Baker Eddy, Winslow Homer, and Julia Ward Howe, who wrote the words to "The Battle Hymn of the Republic."

BOSTON, THE CAPITAL CITY

On warm spring days, the Boston Common comes to life. Teenagers throw frisbees, musicians strum guitars, and couples stroll hand-in-hand along the winding walks that follow ancient cowpaths. Across the street in the Public Garden, swan-shaped boats plow their way around the Frog Pond while tourists snap pictures of the dazzling floral display.

Beginning at the Common, a trail of red bricks set into the

Today, huge modern buildings surround the Old State House (left), one of Boston's most famous landmarks. The Old Granary Burying Ground (above) contains the graves of many prominent early Bostonians.

pavement winds across the city. By following this "Freedom Trail," a sightseer can visit sixteen of Boston's leading historic landmarks. A good place to begin the trail is at the gold-domed "new" State House, designed by Charles Bulfinch in 1795. Then one can go on to the Park Street Church, where William Lloyd Garrison gave his first antislavery speech. Beside the church is the Old Granary Burying Ground, whose weathered headstones bear the names of some of Boston's most renowned citizens, including Declaration of Independence signers John Hancock and Samuel Adams. Further on is the Old South Meeting House, where, on December 16, 1773, a group of angry colonists met before staging the Boston Tea Party. The Old State House, which was the seat of the colonial government, now contains a museum of the city's history. Right outside, a circle of cobblestones marks the site of the Boston Massacre.

A key stop along the Freedom Trail is Faneuil Hall, nicknamed "the Cradle of Liberty" because it was where the colonial patriots

Quincy Market, built in the 1800s as a wholesale meat and produce market, has been renovated into the Faneuil Hall Marketplace, an indoor and outdoor shopping mall complete with food and craft stalls, specialty shops, and restaurants.

met to debate the Stamp Act and the tea tax. Faneuil Hall was donated to the city in 1742 on the condition that it would forever remain a market and a meeting place. Today the lower floor is an emporium of shops and restaurants, while the second story is still used for public meetings and events. Just behind Faneuil Hall are the three granite structures of Quincy Market, which have been renovated into a combination open-air marketplace and indoor shopping mall.

A walk along the Freedom Trail is not complete without a visit to the home of the silversmith who turned patriot, Paul Revere. Nearby stands the Old North Church, where, according to Longfellow's poem, Revere hung a lantern to signal the movements of the British troops before he set out on his gallant ride.

Beyond the Freedom Trail, Boston offers a bounty of treasures to the visitor. On Museum Wharf along the waterfront is the Boston Tea Party Ship and Museum, a floating, full-scale replica of a British East India Company brig. Visitors to the ship are even invited to hurl a few tea chests overboard into Boston Harbor. The nearby Children's Museum contains a variety of hands-on science

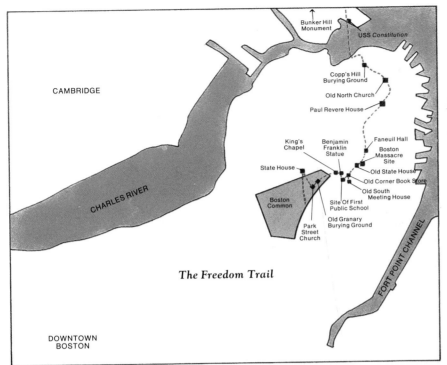

A number of the sites along the Freedom Trail (above) are located in Boston's North End, including Paul Revere's House (right), Boston's oldest standing building; and the Old North Church (above right), the city's oldest church.

exhibits, including a unique display on the history of the computer. Exhibits at the Museum of Afro-American History in the city's Roxbury section depict the long battle black Americans have fought for freedom and civil rights. The Museum of Fine Arts houses a splendid collection of paintings and sculptures from all over the world. It has the world's finest collection of nineteenth-century American Art and one of the world's most complete collections of Asian art. One of Boston's loveliest attractions is the Isabella Stewart Gardner Museum, housed in a stone-by-stone-reconstruction of an Italian Renaissance palazzo.

The walls are covered with lush tapestries and paintings by Rembrandt, Titian, and other masters, and the beautiful interior courtyard is adorned with fresh flowers throughout the year.

Every section of the city yields surprising bits of history or glimpses into ethnic enclaves. The stately mansions on Beacon Hill's Louisburg Square speak of the wealth and tasteful style of the Boston Brahmins. In the North End, Boston's Little Italy, one can wander the narrow, red-brick streets, pausing at colorful shops to sample cannoli or Italian sausage.

As a break from sightseeing, visitors can enjoy elegant shopping along Boylston and Newbury streets in the Back Bay area, or scramble for bargains at famous Filene's Basement, where prices are reduced until the goods are sold. Boston restaurants feature cuisine from every part of the world, but the finest local dishes come from the sea. New England clam chowder is made with a milk base, and connoisseurs emphasize that tomatoes are *never* used. The famous ''Boston scrod'' is actually a tender young codfish—or, as some cooks reluctantly admit, a full-grown codfish cut into small pieces.

While Boston has never lost its reverence for history and culture, it is a city of business and industry as well. Glass-and-steel office buildings line the traffic-choked downtown streets. Commuters pack subways and buses, automobiles pant exhaust fumes, and huge cargo ships unload along the waterfront.

Rising proudly sixty stories above Copley Square is the John Hancock Tower, the tallest building in New England. On a clear day, the view from its crown stretches from Cape Cod to the hills of New Hampshire. At the heart of this panorama lies Boston itself—a landscape of bustling streets and waterways, towers, rooftops, and green patches of parkland—the teeming, pulsing capital of Massachusetts and the largest city in all New England.

Plimouth Plantation near Plymouth is a recreation of the original Pilgrim village as it looked in 1627.

THE SOUTH SHORE AND CAPE COD

While the North Shore is rocky and rugged, the southern arm of Massachusetts Bay, known as the South Shore, is sandy and smooth. One of the most famous towns along the South Shore is Plymouth. For generations, some Americans have claimed special status because their ancestors arrived on the *Mayflower* and became founders of the Plymouth Colony. Most of Plymouth's modern residents are of Portuguese, Italian, or Irish descent. But a few miles from the town itself lies Plimoth Plantation, a reconstruction of the Separatists' original village. The rudely furnished houses and the unadorned church with its rough wooden pews bring to life the familiar story of the Pilgrims' hardships in the New World. Guides in authentic dress speak to visitors in the English dialect of the seventeenth century to convey a real sense of place and time.

Nothing could be a sharper contrast to the pace of downtown Boston than a visit to Cape Cod, about an hour's drive away. Every summer, millions of city-dwellers escape to its sun-dappled beaches to swim and water-ski, fish and sail, or merely to soak up the sun and watch the passing parade of people.

The "Upper Cape," the portion of the cape closest to the

mainland, runs some 30 miles (48 kilometers) east of the Cape Cod Canal. It is an area of low, wooded hills speckled with cranberry bogs and tiny ponds. One of the most interesting features of the Upper Cape is the Woods Hole Oceanographic Institute, which sponsors worldwide research on marine life and topography. One of Woods Hole's research vessels is *Alvin*, a three-man, deep-sea submarine that has helped to map little-known regions of the ocean floor. In 1985, *Alvin* was used to explore the sunken wreck of the *Titanic* in the North Atlantic.

South of the Upper Cape lie the islands of Martha's Vineyard and Nantucket, accessible only by ferry. Both are popular summer resorts, and the few year-round residents grumble about auto-exhaust fumes and traffic jams. Martha's Vineyard has long attracted artists, writers, and celebrities. Among its most prominent residents have been playwright Lillian Hellman and detective-story writer Dashiell Hammett, author of *The Maltese Falcon*. More recently, singer-songwriter Carly Simon has made the Vineyard her summer retreat.

Once the center of the whaling industry, Nantucket sponsors a fascinating whaling museum. Lectures, films, and displays of harpoons and other tools of the trade vividly bring the adventurous days of whaling to life.

At the town of Chatham, the Cape Cod peninsula angles sharply to the north. This region, known as the "Lower Cape," is flat and narrow, a world of sand dunes and bayberry heath where one is never more than 6 miles (9.6 kilometers) from the sea. In 1961, Congress set aside 28,000 acres (11,331 hectares) of this unique habitat as the Cape Cod National Seashore. Every year, millions of nature lovers hike and bicycle along trails through the salt marshes and white-cedar swamps, and watch the flocks of terns, sandpipers, and other birds that nest along the beaches.

In startling contrast is Provincetown, perched on a spit of sand at the Cape's farthest tip. Long established as a fishing village and a haven for artists and writers such as playwright Eugene O'Neill, "P-town" becomes a sprawling playground with every summer season. Commercial Street, the town's main thoroughfare, is lined with gaudy souvenir shops, discotheques, and hot-dog stands. Joggers pound along the beach, swerving through crowds of sunbathers, barking dogs, and children building sand castles.

What would the Pilgrims think of all this flagrant pleasure seeking if they could see Provincetown today? In November of 1620, more than a month before they reached Plymouth, the *Mayflower's* passengers clambered ashore here to explore the tip of Cape Cod. Today, within earshot of Commercial Street's discos, the 252-foot (77-meter) spire of the Pilgrim Monument commemorates their historic visit.

Perhaps this is a fitting spot to end this brief tour of Massachusetts—the site where those long-ago colonists first touched North American soil and began to shape its history. At Provincetown, as in so many towns throughout Massachusetts, the past and present have an exciting way of coming together.

FACTS AT A GLANCE

GENERAL INFORMATION

Statehood: February 6, 1788, sixth state

Origin of Name: Named for an Indian tribe called the Massachusett that lived in the Massachusetts Bay area; the name is believed to mean "near the great hill," probably referring to the Great Blue Hill south of Boston

State Capital: Boston, founded 1630

State Nickname: The "Bay State" (the state's official name is the Commonwealth of Massachusetts)

State Flag: The state flag was adopted in 1908. A gold Indian holding a bow in his right hand and an arrow in his left hand is depicted on a blue shield against a white background. The arrow is pointing downward to symbolize peace. Above the shield, a bent arm holding a sword symbolizes the state motto, which is written out on a banner flowing around the shield.

State Motto: *Ense petit placidam sub libertate quietem,* (By the sword we seek peace, but peace only with liberty)

State Bird: Chickadee

State Flower: Mayflower (trailing arbutus)

State Tree: American elm

State Insect: Ladybug

State Horse: Morgan horse

State Beverage: Cranberry juice

State Fish: Cod

State Song: "All Hail to Massachusetts," words and music by Arthur J. Marsh; adopted as the official state song in 1966:

All hail to Massachusetts, the land of the free and the brave!
For Bunker Hill and Charlestown, and flag we love to wave:
For Lexington and Concord, and the shot heard 'round the world:
All hail to Massachusetts, we'll keep her flag unfurled.
She stands upright for freedom's light that shines from sea to sea:
All hail to Massachusetts! Our country 'tis of thee!

All hail to grand old Bay State, the home of the bean and the cod!
Where pilgrims found a landing and gave their thanks to God.
A land of opportunity in the good old U.S.A.
Where men live long and prosper, and people come to stay.
Don't sell her short but learn to court her industry and stride:
All hail to grand old Bay State! The land of pilgrim's pride!

All hail to Massachusetts, renowned in the Hall of Fame!
How proudly wave her banner emblazoned with her name!
In unity and brotherhood, sons and daughters go hand in hand:
All hail to Massachusetts, there is no finer land!
It's M-A-S-S-A-C-H-U-S-E-T-T-S.
All hail to Massachusetts! All hail! All hail! All hail!

POPULATION

Population: 5,737,081, eleventh among the states (1980 census)

Population Density: 693 people per sq. mi. (268 people per km^2)

Population Distribution: 84 percent of the people live in cities or towns. Boston, Massachusetts' capital, ranks seventh in population in the United States and first among the six New England states

Boston	562,994
Worcester	161,799
Springfield	152,319
New Bedford	98,478
Cambridge	95,322
Brockton	95,172
Fall River	92,574
Lowell	92,418
Quincy	84,743
Newton	83,622
Lynn	78,471

Population Growth: Massachusetts' greatest population increase, 35 percent, took place between 1840 and 1850. Except for the Civil-War period in the 1860s,

Massachusetts' population grew an average of 20 percent between each census until 1910, when many factories began fleeing the state to relocate to places where labor and operating costs were lower. The need for new industries and new technologies created by World War II helped revitalize the Massachusetts economy. From 1970 to 1980, however, the state's population grew by just .8 percent, compared to the national growth rate of 11.45 percent. The list below shows population growth in Massachusetts since 1820:

Year	Population
1820	523,287
1840	737,699
1860	1,231,066
1880	1,783,085
1900	2,805,346
1920	3,852,366
1940	4,316,721
1950	4,690,514
1960	5,148,578
1970	5,689,170
1980	5,737,081

GEOGRAPHY

Borders: States that border Massachusetts are Vermont and New Hampshire on the north, New York on the west, and Rhode Island and Connecticut on the south. The Atlantic Ocean forms the state's eastern border and part of its southern border.

Highest Point: Mount Greylock in Berkshire County, 3,491 ft. (1,064 m)

Lowest Point: Sea level, along the Atlantic Ocean

Greatest Distances: North to south—110 mi. (177 km)
East to west—190 mi. (306 km)

Area: 8,284 sq. mi. (21,456 km²)

Rank in Area Among the States: Forty-fifth

Rivers: Western Massachusetts is drained by the Berkshire Valley rivers: the Hoosic River flows northwest into Vermont, emptying into the Hudson River, and the Housatonic River winds south into Connecticut. The Connecticut River flows through west-central Massachusetts and is the state's longest and most important waterway. Its main tributaries are the Deerfield, Westfield, Chicopee, and Millers rivers. The Blackstone River passes through Worcester in its southeastward path to Rhode Island. The Taunton empties into Mount Hope Bay at Fall River. In northeastern Massachusetts, the Merrimack River enters the state from New Hampshire, and flows northeastward to empty into the Atlantic Ocean. Three noted rivers that empty into Boston Harbor are the Charles, Mystic, and Neponset.

Nauset Marsh, part of Cape Cod National Seashore

Lakes: Massachusetts has more than thirteen hundred lakes and ponds. The two largest lakes are man-made reservoirs in central Massachusetts: Quabbin (39 sq. mi./101 km²) near Ware, and Wachusett (6.5 sq. mi./17 km²) near Worcester. Assawompset Pond in southern Massachusetts is the state's largest natural lake. Massachusetts' best-known body of water, however, is probably tiny Walden Pond in Concord, the famous retreat of Henry David Thoreau.

Topography: Massachusetts may be divided into six geographic regions.

The Taconic Range is a narrow strip, less than six mi. (ten km) wide, along Massachusetts' western border. Mount Greylock rises to 3,491 ft. (1,064 m) in the north; Mount Everett reaches 2,602 ft. (793 m) in the south.

The Berkshire Valley, less than ten mi. (sixteen km) at its widest point, is hemmed in by the Taconic Range to the west and the Berkshire Hills to the east.

The part of the Western New England Upland that stretches across Massachusetts is known as the Berkshire Hills. The Berkshires are an extension of the Green Mountains of Vermont. The region consists of a number of ranges and small valleys stretching 20-30 mi. (32-48 km) between the Berkshire Valley on the west and the Connecticut River Valley on the east. Its highest point is Spruce Hill (2,588 ft./789 m) in the Hoosac Range.

The Connecticut River Valley broadens from a width of three mi. (five km) in the northern part of the state to a width of twenty mi. (thirty-two km) in the south. It provides the main drainage for most of the upland regions of Massachusetts. Its open meadows and fertile soil, tinted red by the sandstone hills, make it the richest agricultural area in the state.

The Eastern New England Upland occupies the 40-60 mi. (64-97 km) stretch of land between the Connecticut River Valley and the Coastal Lowlands. This hilly plateau is characterized by numerous small streams and by monadnocks (isolated hills of hard, erosion-resistant rock).

The Coastal Lowlands occupy the eastern third of Massachusetts and include the Cape Cod peninsula, the offshore islands of Nantucket and Martha's Vineyard, the Elizabeth Islands, and the area 30-50 mi. (48-80.5 km) inland from the ragged coastline along the Atlantic Ocean. The region is rugged and hilly in the north, then slopes down to the grasslands, sandy beaches, and cranberry bogs of Cape Cod.

Climate: Massachusetts' climate is temperate, but frequent weather changes are common. Within the state, cold and dry air from the north meet warm and moist air from the south to create storms called "nor'easters." Tropical hurricanes may hit the coast in late summer or early fall. Eastern Massachusetts has both warmer winters and warmer summers than western Massachusetts. Boston, on the east coast, averages 29° F. (-1.7° C) in January, while Pittsfield, in western Berkshire County, averages 21° F. (-6° C). Boston's average July temperature is 72° F. (22° C), and Pittsfield's is 68° F. (20° C). The lowest-recorded temperature in the state was -34° F. (-37° C) at Birch Hill Dam on January 18, 1957; the highest recorded temperature was 107° F. (42° C) at Chester and New Bedford on August 2, 1975. Eastern Massachusetts receives an average of 40 in. (102 cm) of rain and 42 in. (107 cm) of snow annually. Western Massachusetts receives more precipitation, averaging 44 in. (112 cm) of rain and 55-75 in. (140-192 cm) of snow annually.

NATURE

Trees: Oak, hickory, ash, beech, maple, birch, eastern hemlock, eastern white pine, red pine, pitch pine

Wild Plants: Aster, trailing arbutus, skunk cabbage, goldenrod, white hellebore, marsh marigold, Solomon's seal, lady's slipper, trillium, azalea, dogwood, violet, mountain laurel, shadbush and viburnum shrubs, varieties of fern, coastal grasses, rushes, and sedges

Animals: Deer, bats, beavers, chipmunks, meadow mice, foxes, moles, raccoons, muskrats, porcupines, rabbits, shrews, bears, skunks, snakes, squirrels, coyotes, weasels, woodchucks

Birds: Blue jays, cardinals, mallard ducks, grouse, gulls, bald eagles, mockingbirds, owls, partridges, pheasant, quails, terns, woodpeckers

Fish: Freshwater fish include bass, bullhead, carp, white and yellow perch, pickerel, sunfish, and trout; on the coast are ocean fish, clams, lobsters, mussels, and oysters

GOVERNMENT

The government of Massachusetts, like that of the federal government, is divided into three branches—legislative, executive, and judicial. The state's legislative branch is called the General Court. It is made up of a senate with 40 members and a house of representatives with 160 members. The General Court creates new laws, rescinds or revises old ones, and works with the state governor to prepare the state budget. Voters elect both senators and representatives to two-year terms.

The executive branch, headed by the governor, administers the law. The governor and lieutenant governor are elected to four-year terms. There is no limit to the number of terms a governor may serve. The state constitution gives the governor the power to veto or approve laws passed by the General Court, to serve as commander-in-chief of the state militia, and to call emergency sessions of the General Court. An elected Executive Council, composed of eight members, has power of approval over such matters as pardons and judicial appointments.

The judicial branch interprets laws and tries cases. The state has three kinds of courts—supreme, appellate, and trial. All judges are appointed by the governor, subject to the approval of the Executive Council. Judges serve for ten years or until they turn seventy, whichever is later. The state's highest court is the supreme judicial court. It has a chief justice and six associate justices. The appeals court, which hears appeals of criminal and civil cases, has a chief justice and ten associate justices. The main trial court is called the superior court. It has a chief justice and sixty associate justices. The district and municipal courts are the lowest courts in Massachusetts.

Number of Counties: 14

U.S. Representatives: 11

Electoral Votes: 13

EDUCATION

The state's public school system, established in 1647, is the nation's oldest. In 1983-84, Massachusetts spent an average of $3,378 for each of the 878,844 pupils enrolled in the state's 1,827 public elementary and secondary schools. Massachusetts has some of the nation's most famous private preparatory schools. Included among these are Phillip's Andover, Deerfield, Northfield-Mount Hermon, Milton, and Groton.

Massachusetts is also noted for its many institutions of higher learning. There are about 120 colleges and universities in the state; three-fourths of them are private institutions. The state's largest public university is the University of Massachusetts, which has a main campus in Amherst, a Boston campus, and a medical school in Worcester. Other public universities include Southeastern Massachusetts University in North Dartmouth and the University of Lowell in Lowell. Massachusetts state colleges are located at Boston, Bridgewater, Fitchburg, Framingham, Lowell, North Adams, Salem, Westfield, and Worcester. The Massachusetts Board of Regional Community Colleges oversees fifteen campuses. Among private schools of higher learning, Harvard University in Cambridge is the nation's oldest and one of the most prestigious. The Massachusetts Institute of Technology, also in Cambridge, is one of the nation's top science and engineering schools. Private schools in Boston include Boston University, Northeastern University, Simmons College, New England Conservatory of Music, and Boston Conservatory. Other noted Massachusetts colleges and universities are Amherst College and Hampshire College in Amherst, Boston College in Chestnut Hill, Tufts University in Medford, Brandeis University in Waltham, Clark University and College of the Holy Cross in Worcester, Mount Holyoke College in South Hadley, Wheaton College in Norton, Smith College in Northampton, Wellesley College in Wellesley, and Williams College in Williamstown.

ECONOMY AND INDUSTRY

Principal Products:
Agriculture: Greenhouse and nursery specialties, dairy products, cranberries, eggs, beef cattle, hogs, apples, hay, asparagus, cucumbers, tomatoes, corn, potatoes, cigar tobacco, strawberries

Manufacturing: Nonelectric machinery, electric and electronic equipment, instruments, fabricated metal products, paper, rubber, plastic, leather products, textiles, food products, chemicals, primary metals, glass products, toys, sporting goods, printing and publishing

Natural Resources: Building stone, sand and gravel, lime, clay, offshore fishing grounds, good harbors

Business, Industry, and Trade: Service industries are the mainstay of Massachusetts' economy, making up 71 percent of the gross state product (GSP) — the total value of goods and services produced annually. Manufacturing is the next most important economic activity, accounting for 25 percent of the GSP. Massachusetts is a major printing and publishing center. A large number of electronics research-and-development facilities, computer and computer component producers, and other high-technology firms are concentrated around Boston. Boston is New England's wholesale and retail trading center. It is the world's second-busiest wholesale wool market and is a major fish market. Tourism is an important business thoughout the state. In 1983, almost 9 million people visited Massachusetts' national parks and historic sites and some 11.5 million visited state parks and recreation areas.

Finance: Massachusetts has more than 130 commercial banks and about 150 savings and loan associations. Boston is New England's financial center, and is the location of the First Federal Reserve District Bank. The Boston Stock Exchange, founded in 1846, is a major stock exchange. Massachusetts is also an important insurance center.

Communication: Massachusetts has about 240 newspapers, about 45 daily newspapers, and about 400 periodicals. The most important newspapers are the *Boston Globe,* the *Boston Herald,* and the *Christian Science Monitor,* all in Boston; the *Worcester Telegram and Gazette;* the *Springfield Union;* the *Springfield Daily News;* the *Patriot Ledger* in Quincy; the *Berkshire Eagle* in Pittsfield; and the *Standard Times* in New Bedford. The Boston-based magazine *Atlantic Monthly* is the oldest literary magazine in the United States. Massachusetts has 123 radio stations and 14 television stations. WGBH in Boston is a major producer of programming for the Public Broadcasting Service.

Transportation: Massachusetts has about 25 public airports and about 135 private airports. Logan International Airport in Boston, the state's largest and busiest airport, is served by more than twenty-five airlines. Massachusetts has 1,650 mi. (2,660 km) of railroad track, and about 33,800 mi. (54,400 km) of roads and highways. Boston is New England's major seaport. It handles about 20 million tons (18 million metric tons) of cargo a year. Fall River and Salem are other important ports.

SOCIAL AND CULTURAL LIFE

Museums: Boston, a major educational and cultural center, abounds with museums. The Boston Museum of Fine Arts is one of the world's leading museums, with outstanding collections in Asian art, Egyptian art, French Impressionism, and American art and furniture. The Isabella Stewart Gardner Museum features art housed in a beautiful Italian-Renaissance-style palazzo. The Institute of Contemporary Art features twentieth-century works. The Boston Children's Museum features many "hands-on" exhibits. The New England Aquarium has two thousand species of marine life from around the world. The Museum of Science includes the Charles Hayden Planetarium, and features more than four hundred exhibits ranging from astronomy to zoology.

Across the river in Cambridge, Harvard University's museums include the Busch-Reisinger Museum, the Fogg Art Museum, the Sackler Art Museum, the Peabody Museum of Archaeology and Ethnology, the Mineralogical Museum, the Museum of Comparative Zoology, and the Botanical Museum.

Other Massachusetts museums of note are the Worcester Art Museum, the DeCordova and Dana Museum and Park in Lincoln, the National Marine Fisheries Aquarium in Woods Hole, the Springfield Science Museum, and the Berkshire Natural Museum in Pittsfield. Salem has a number of interesting historical museums, including the Salem Witch Museum, which vividly recreates the story of the Salem witchcraft trials; the Peabody Museum, a maritime and natural history museum; and the Essex Institute, a complex of six restored early-American homes. Other specialized museums include the Concord Antiquarian Museum, the Sandwich Glass Museum, the Museum of American Textile History in North Andover, the New Bedford Whaling Museum, the Whaling Museum in Nantucket, the John Woodman Higgins Armory in Worcester, and the American Clock and Watch Museum in Bristol.

Libraries: The Boston Public Library, with 28 branches and more than 4.5 million volumes, is Massachusetts' largest public library. Founded in 1854, it is the oldest major public library in the United States. The Worcester Public Library has six branches and more than 850,000 volumes. The Springfield Public Library has eight branches and more than 650,000 volumes. The Boston Athenaeum, a private library that holds 600,000 volumes, is the best-known private library in the state. The American Antiquarian Society in Worcester has the world's largest collection of early-American newspapers, sheet music, children's books, and other printed matter. Other outstanding collections are owned by the Massachusetts Historical Society Library, the state library in the Massachusetts State House, and the New England Historic Genealogical Society, all in Boston. The Harvard University library system, with nearly 10 million volumes, is the largest and one of the best university libraries in the world. The John Fitzgerald Kennedy Library in Dorchester houses the papers and other memorabilia of the thirty-fifth president of the United States.

Performing Arts: The Boston Symphony Orchestra has long been one of America's preeminent musical organizations. In the summer the orchestra moves to Tanglewood in the Berkshire Hills of western Massachusetts. The Boston Pops Orchestra specializes in lighter works and is composed of players from the Boston

A crew race on the Charles River

Symphony. Other musical organizations include the Handel and Hayden Society, the Civic Symphony, the Pro Arte Chamber Orchestra, the American Vocal Arts Quintet, and the Boston Opera Company under the direction of Sarah Caldwell.

The Boston Ballet performs new and traditional works at the Wang Center of the Performing Arts. The Concert Dance Company of Boston and the Mark Morris Dance Company present contemporary works. The Jacob's Pillow Dance Festival is held every summer in Lee in the Berkshires.

Many plays open in Boston before going on to New York. Three theaters that present pre-Broadway premieres are the Shubert, the Wilbur, and the Colonial. The Boston area also has a number of repertory groups, including the American Repertory Theatre, the Boston Shakespeare Company, and the Huntington Theater Company. Other Boston theaters include Next Move, the Charles Playhouse, Lyric State, and Theater Works. Dozens of community and college theater groups in the Greater Boston area, including Harvard's Loeb Drama Center, present plays. Some of the finest summer theater in the country can be seen at the Williamstown Theater Festival. The Berkshire Theater Festival in Stockbridge presents American classics and new works by American playwrights.

Sports and Recreation: Boston is represented by a team in every major professional sport. The Boston Red Sox of baseball's American League play in Fenway Park, one of the nation's oldest and best-loved ballparks. The Boston Celtics, the National Basketball Association's most successful team, play on the famous parquet floor at the Boston Garden. The Boston Bruins of the National Hockey League also play at the Boston Garden. The New England Patriots of the National Football League play in Sullivan Stadium in Foxboro, just south of Boston.

One can watch Thoroughbred horse racing at Suffolk Downs in East Boston, and greyhound racing at both the Taunton Dog Track in North Dighton and at Wonderland Park in Revere. The Boston Marathon, first run in 1897, is America's oldest and most famous marathon race. Held each year on Patriot's Day, the third Monday in April, it attracts runners from all over the world.

The Atlantic Ocean and the hundreds of lakes, rivers, streams, and ponds in Massachusetts provide excellent fishing, boating, and swimming. Massachusetts has 107 state parks, forests, and recreational areas where hunting, camping, hiking, skating, cross-country and downhill skiing, and other kinds of outdoor recreation are possible. Boston has nine public beaches and more than 4,500 acres (1,820 hectares) of public parks. Cape Cod National Seashore and the nearby islands of Martha's Vineyard and Nantucket are noted for their splendid beaches. In central Massachusetts, the Tully Lake Recreation Area provides wilderness camping, canoeing, fishing, hiking, horseback trails, and hunting. The Quabbin Back Country west of Worcester teems with wildlife. In Western Massachusetts, one can walk 80 mi. (129 km) of the Appalachian Trail that runs from Maine to Georgia. There is downhill skiing at East Mountain State Recreation in Great Barrington, cross-country skiing at Mount Greylock State Reservation in Lanesboro, and six different bicycle trails in the Pioneer Valley region.

Historic Sites and Landmarks:

Adams National Historic Site in Quincy is the 1731 home of four generations of the Adams family, including John Adams and John Quincy Adams, the second and sixth presidents of the United States.

Boston National Historic Park occupies 41 acres (16.5 hectares) of the city. A 2.5-mi. (4-km) "Freedom Trail" starts on the *Boston Common*, the oldest public park in the United States, and ends at *Bunker Hill*, where a monument commemorates the 1775 victory of the patriots over the British. Included along the way are visits to fourteen other sites of historic eighteenth- and nineteenth-century Boston: the "new" *State House*, designed in 1795 by noted architect Charles Bulfinch; *Park Street Church*, where William Lloyd Garrison gave his first anti-slavery address; *Old Granary Burying Ground*, where John Hancock, Samuel Adams, Paul Revere, victims of the Boston Massacre, and other notable Bay Staters are buried; *King's Chapel*, the first Episcopal church in Boston and later the first Unitarian church in the United States; *Benjamin Franklin Statue* and *Site of Boston Latin School*, the first public secondary school in the American colonies; *Old Corner Bookstore*, which became Boston's literary salon and served as a meeting place for Longfellow, Emerson, Hawthorne, Thoreau, Holmes, and other writers; *Old South Meeting House*, where colonists met before launching the Boston Tea Party; *Old State House*, the seat of the colonial government of Massachusetts; *Boston Massacre Site*; *Faneuil Hall*, the meeting hall and market where patriots of the American Revolution met; *Paul Revere House*, Boston's oldest structure and Revere's home from 1770 to 1780; *Old North Church*, in whose steeple two signal lanterns were lit to warn patriots in Charlestown that the British were coming; *Copp's Hill Burying Ground*, which contains the graves of Cotton Mather and other early Bostonians; and *Charles Navy Yard* in Charlestown, home of the USS *Constitution* ("Old Ironsides"), the world's oldest commissioned warship still afloat.

Lowell National Historical Park in Lowell preserves the factory buildings, dormitories, and row houses that made up America's first planned industrial community.

John F. Kennedy National Historic Site in Brookline is the birthplace of the thirty-fifth president of the United States.

Longfellow National Historic Site in Cambridge is the Georgian-style house where Henry Wadsworth Longfellow lived for forty-five years while writing some of his most famous poetry. George Washington had used the house as his headquarters from 1775 to 1776 during the siege of Boston.

Lowell National Historical Park in Lowell, which commemorates Francis Cabot Lowell's role in the Industrial Revolution, is the site of the first planned industrial community in the United States.

Minute Man National Historical Park in Concord is a 750-acre (303-hectare) park near Concord that includes Daniel Chester French's statue *The Minute Man,* as well as a reconstruction of the North Bridge where the minutemen stood their ground when the first shots of the Revolution were fired.

Frederick Law Olmsted National Historic Site in Brookline was the home and office of the nineteenth-century landscape architect who designed some of the country's greatest parks, including New York's Central Park and the string of six parks in Boston known as the "Emerald Necklace."

Salem Maritime National Historic Site in Salem contains the waterfront wharves and buildings from Salem's years as a leading American seaport. Included are the 1819 Custom House, Derby Wharf, Bonded Warehouse, and the West India Goods Store.

Saugus Iron Works National Historic Site in Saugus is a reconstruction of the 1643 ironworks founded by John Winthrop Jr., son of Governor John Winthrop. It includes a restored ironmaster's house, a museum with artifacts, and a working blacksmith shop.

Springfield Armory in Springfield was founded in 1777 during the revolutionary war. It was used for the manufacture of weapons until 1968, when it became a National Historic Site.

119

The *Mayflower II* is a full-scale replica of the ship that brought the Pilgrims to America in 1620.

Other Interesting Places to Visit:

Black Heritage Trail in Boston is a walking tour that explores the history of Beacon Hill's nineteenth-century black community. Included on the tour are the African Meeting House, the oldest black church building still standing in the United States; the Smith Court Residences, five homes typical of those lived in by nineteenth-century black Bostonians; the George Middleton House, built in 1797 and one of the oldest homes on Beacon Hill; and the Lewis and Harriet Hayden House on Phillips Street, which was at one time used to harbor slaves and was once visited by Harriet Beecher Stowe.

Ralph Waldo Emerson House in Concord, where Emerson lived from 1835 until his death in 1882, was built by the writer himself in 1820. The house has been restored to look as it did when he lived there, and still contains his well-stocked library of classics and first editions.

Hancock Shaker Village in Hancock is a restoration of a nineteenth-century village built and inhabited by people of the Shaker religious sect.

Historic Deerfield was the last outpost of New England's frontier when it was settled in 1669. Today twelve museum-houses display the history of Deerfield and the culture of the Connecticut River Valley.

Old Manse in Concord, the home of Ralph Waldo Emerson's family, was built in 1765 by Reverend William Emerson, the poet's grandfather. The house was later lived in by Nathaniel Hawthorne.

Old Sturbridge Village in Sturbridge features more than forty restored buildings on 200 acres (81 hectares) of rolling land. Costumed guides demonstrate activities from the daily lives of people in a typical New England village of the early 1800s.

Plymouth Rock, now protected by a granite monument, is where the Pilgrims chose to come ashore after scouting the area for a month following their initial landfall at Provincetown.

Orchard House in Concord, the second home of the family of Louisa May Alcott, was where the author wrote the first part of *Little Women*. Preserved here are Alcott furnishings, books, and pictures.

Plimoth Plantation, near Plymouth, is a recreation of the original Pilgrim village as it looked in 1627. The authenticity is enhanced by men and women in period dress who answer visitors' questions in seventeenth-century dialect.

Plymouth Rock in Plymouth is where the Pilgrims chose to come ashore after scouting the area for a month following their landfall at Provincetown. Nearby is the *Mayflower II*, a replica of the ship that brought the Pilgrims to America.

Sleepy Hollow Cemetery in Concord contains the graves of Thoreau, Emerson, the Alcott family, Hawthorne, and other famous Bay Staters.

Walden Pond, near Concord, is where writer Henry David Thoreau built a cabin and lived alone from 1845 to 1847. Visitors can fish, swim, and picnic at the pond.

Witch House in Salem, a restored seventeenth-century house, was once the residence of Jonathan Corwin, one of the witchcraft-trial judges.

121

IMPORTANT DATES

1500s — Algonquian tribes living in Massachusetts include the Massachusett, Nauset, Nipmuc, Pennacook, Pocomtuc, and Wampanoag

1602 — English explorer Bartholomew Gosnold visits Massachusetts and names its peninsula Cape Cod

1620 — Pilgrims arriving on the *Mayflower* found Plymouth Colony

1621 — Pilgrims celebrate the first Thanksgiving

1630 — Puritans found Massachusetts Bay Colony at Boston

1635 — Boston Latin School, the first public secondary school in the American colonies, opens

1636 — First college in the colonies (later named Harvard) is established at New Towne (Cambridge)

1647 — Massachusetts establishes a system of public education

1675-78 — King Philip's War

1684 — Massachusetts' charter is revoked when the British Crown establishes the Dominion of New England to regain some control over the colony

1691 — England grants a new charter to Massachusetts combining the Plymouth and Massachusetts Bay into one colony

1692 — Witch hunts and witchcraft trials disrupt Salem and neighboring towns; nineteen people are hanged

1704 — The French and their Indian allies attack Deerfield, burning the town, killing 49 people, and carrying 110 more to captivity in Canada; the colonies' first successful newspaper, the *Boston News-Letter*, appears

1764 — England stirs up colonial resentment by passing the Revenue Act, which taxes sugar imported into the colonies

1765 — American colonists are further outraged by passage of the Stamp Act

1767 — England passes the Townshend Acts, which tax glass, lead, paint, and tea coming into the colonies; the colonists decide to boycott British goods

1768 — British troops arrive in Boston

1770 — In what becomes known as the Boston Massacre, British troops fire into a crowd of angry colonists, killing five people

1773—In what becomes known as the Boston Tea Party, colonists dump British tea into Boston Harbor to protest the Tea Act

1775—Paul Revere makes his famous ride to warn the colonial militia that the British are about to attack; the revolutionary war begins at Lexington and Concord; the British defeat the colonists in the Battle of Bunker Hill

1776—Massachusetts unanimously approves the Declaration of Independence; the British are driven out of Boston

1780—The Massachusetts State Constitution, containing a Bill of Rights, is ratified; John Hancock is elected governor

1786-87—Shays' Rebellion

1788—Massachusetts becomes the sixth state to enter the Union

1797—John Adams becomes the second president of the United States; the United States Frigate *Constitution* ("Old Ironsides") is launched at Boston

1807—The Embargo Act ends foreign trade, devastating Massachusetts' shipping industry

1815—Francis Cabot Lowell opens a textile mill in Waltham

1822—Boston is incorporated as a city

1824—John Quincy Adams is elected sixth president of the United States

1837—Mary Lyon founds Mount Holyoke College in South Hadley, the first women's college in the United States

1869—The last whaler sails from New Bedford; Massachusetts establishes the nation's first state board of health

1897—Boston opens the nation's first subway; first Boston Marathon is held

1912—Lawrence textile workers and Boston streetcar operators go on strike

1919—Governor Calvin Coolidge receives nationwide attention for calling in state police to break the Boston police strike

1923—Vice-President Calvin Coolidge of Northampton becomes the fifteenth president of the United States when President Harding dies in office

1927—Nicola Sacco and Bartolomeo Vanzetti, Italian-born anarchists who were convicted in 1921 for murder committed in South Braintree in 1920, are executed

1942—Fire kills 491 people at Boston's Cocoanut Grove Nightclub

1960—John F. Kennedy is elected thirty-fifth president of the United States

1974—A federal court orders busing of students to achieve immediate racial desegregation in Boston schools

1976—In the biggest oil-spill disaster in American history, some 5 million gallons (22.7 million) of oil damage Nantucket and Cape Cod beaches and threaten what are the world's richest commercial fishing grounds

1980—Massachusetts voters approve Proposition 2½, a tax-cutting referendum that will result in lay-offs for thousands of teachers and other state workers

1985—Dr. Laval S. Wilson becomes the first black superintendent of Boston's public school system

1986—Harvard celebrates its 350th birthday

1988—Governor Michael S. Dukakis signs the Health Security Act bill; this law ensures that all Massachusetts residents will have access to affordable health care by 1992

1990—Dr. Joseph Murray shares the Nobel Prize in Physiology or Medicine for his discoveries in organ transplants

IMPORTANT PEOPLE

JOHN QUINCY ADAMS

SAMUEL ADAMS

John Adams (1735-1826), born in Braintree (now Quincy); patriot, lawyer, and second president of the United States; delegate to Continental Congress; helped draft the Declaration of Independence and the 1780 Massachusetts State Constitution; helped negotiate peace treaty with Great Britain at end of revolutionary war; first vice-president of the United States under George Washington (1789-97); president of the United States (1797-1801)

John Quincy Adams (1767-1848), born in Braintree (now Quincy), son of John Adams; sixth president of the United States; United States senator (1803-08); participated in the negotiations that settled the War of 1812; secretary of state under President Monroe (1817-25); president of the United States (1825-29), United States Representative (1831-48)

Samuel Adams (1722-1803), born in Boston; patriot; the leading agitator in the fight for American independence; member of Massachusetts legislature (1765-74); organized opposition to the Stamp Act; organized the Boston Tea Party; delegate to the Continental congresses; signer of the Declaration of Independence; helped draft the Massachusetts State Constitution; lieutenant governor of Massachusetts (1789-93); governor of Massachusetts (1794-97)

Louisa May Alcott (1832-1888); author who grew up in the Boston area; wrote a number of popular novels, including *Little Women*, one of America's best-loved children's books

Horatio Alger (1832-1899), born in Revere; clergyman and author; wrote more than a hundred popular novels about poor, sometimes homeless boys who rose from "rags to riches"

Susan Brownell Anthony (1820-1906), born in Adams; social reformer; participated in the abolition and temperance movements; won national and international recognition for her tireless efforts to achieve woman suffrage

Crispus Attucks (1723?-1770), born in Framingham; patriot; was the first to fall when British troops fired upon a mob of angry colonists in 1770 during the Boston Massacre

William Bradford (1590-1657); Pilgrim leader; sailed to America on the *Mayflower*; became second governor of the Plymouth Colony in 1621 and led it successfully through crises of famine, debt, and Indian hostilities; served intermittently as governor until 1657

Anne Dudley Bradstreet (1612?-1672); poet; considered the first American poet of merit; settled in Massachusetts in 1630; wrote the first published collection of original poetry from the American colonies, *The Tenth Muse Lately Sprung Up in America*

Louis Dembitz Brandeis (1856-1941); lawyer and jurist; graduate of Harvard Law School; concerned with social reform, especially economic and political rights for working people; also noted for his devotion to the principle of free speech; associate justice of the United States Supreme Court (1916-39)

Edward William Brooke (1919-   ); lawyer and political leader; as Massachusetts attorney general (1963-67), gained nationwide attention for his exposure of corruption in the state government; United States senator (1967-79)

William Cullen Bryant (1794-1878), born in Cummington; poet and editor; the leading American poet of the 1820s and 1830s; in 1829 became co-owner and editor of the *New York Evening Post*

Charles Bulfinch (1763-1844), born in Boston; considered America's first professional architect; built elegant private homes; designed the Massachusetts State House, Boston's New South Church, the Beacon Hill Monument, and other public buildings

George Herbert Walker Bush (1924-   ), born in Milton; forty-first president of the United States (1989-   ); distinguished U.S. Navy pilot during World War II; settled in Texas, where he helped found the Zapata Petroleum Corporation (1953); director of the Central Intelligence Agency (1976-77); vice-president under President Ronald Reagan (1981-89)

Sarah Caldwell (1924-   ); musician; artistic director, conductor, and founder of The Opera Company of Boston

LOUISA MAY ALCOTT

SUSAN B. ANTHONY

LOUIS BRANDEIS

WM. CULLEN BRYANT

CALVIN COOLIDGE

EMILY DICKINSON

W. E. B. DUBOIS

MARY BAKER EDDY

John Cheever (1912-1982), born in Quincy; writer; portrayed suburban, upper-middle-class American life; won the 1979 Pulitzer Prize in fiction for *The Stories of John Cheever*

Calvin Coolidge (1872-1933); thirtieth president of the United States; governor of Massachusetts (1919-21); vice-president under President Warren G. Harding (1921-23); president (1923-29)

John Singleton Copley (1738-1815), born in Boston; artist; considered the finest portrait painter of his day; noted for portraying his subjects with a realism that was unusual for the time

James Michael Curley (1874-1958), born in Boston; politician; Irish-American who dominated Boston politics in the first half of the twentieth century; mayor of Boston (1914-18, 1922-26, 1930-34, 1946-50); governor of Massachusetts (1935-37); was accused of widespread corruption; used patronage and other machine-politics tactics to achieve political success

Emily Elizabeth Dickinson (1830-1886), born in Amherst; poet; became acclaimed as one of America's finest poets when her poems were discovered and published after her death

Dorothea Lynde Dix (1802-1887); reformer and philanthropist; grew up in Massachusetts; crusaded to improve prison conditions and to build state hospitals for the mentally ill

William Edward Burghardt (W.E.B.) DuBois (1868-1963), born in Great Barrington; educator, historian, sociologist, and civil-rights leader; believed blacks would achieve social and political equality only through education, working together, and strongly protesting discrimination; in 1910 helped found the National Association for the Advancement of Colored People (NAACP)

Mary Baker Eddy (1821-1910), born near Concord; founder of the Church of Christ, Scientist; studied the Bible and developed a philosophy of spiritual healing; wrote the Christian Science textbook *Science and Health with Key to the Scriptures*; founded the daily newspaper *The Christian Science Monitor*

Jonathan Edwards (1703-1758); Congregational minister; considered one of the greatest American Puritan theologians; in the 1740s, his powerful preaching stimulated the New England-wide religious revival known as "The Great Awakening"

John Eliot (1604-1690); Puritan missionary and teacher at Roxbury; learned an Algonquian dialect in order to preach to the Indians; in 1651 organized the first of fourteen "praying towns" of Indian converts; prepared the first books printed in an American Indian language

Ralph Waldo Emerson (1803-1882), born in Boston; philosopher; former Unitarian minister; became one of the most influential and popular lecturers, essayists, and poets of his time; developed the transcendentalist philosophy

Arthur Fiedler (1894-1979), born in Boston; conductor; led the Boston Pops Orchestra from 1930 to 1979

Felix Frankfurter (1882-1965), jurist, scholar; Harvard Law School professor (1914-39); helped found the American Civil Liberties Union; advised President Franklin D. Roosevelt on much of the New Deal legislation; associate justice of the United States Supreme Court (1939-62); received the Presidential Medal of Freedom (1963)

Benjamin Franklin (1706-1790), born in Boston; left at the age of seventeen after several years of apprenticeship as a printer to his brother James; settled in Philadelphia; achieved international fame as a patriot, statesman, diplomat, inventor, and author

Daniel Chester French (1850-1931), sculptor; worked in Boston and Concord from 1878 to 1887; first important commission was *The Minute Man*, to commemorate the hundredth anniversary of the Battle at Concord; also created the seated statue of Lincoln in the Lincoln Memorial in Washington D.C.

William Lloyd Garrison (1805-1879), born in Newburyport; journalist and reformer; leader of radical abolitionists; published the weekly antislavery paper *The Liberator*; founded the American Anti-Slavery Society

John Hancock (1737-1793), born in Braintree (now Quincy); patriot and politician; played a major role in many of the events that led up to the revolutionary war; member of the Massachusetts legislature (1769-74); member of the Continental Congress (1775-80); first man to sign the Declaration of Independence

John Harvard (1609-1638); Puritan clergyman who came to Massachusetts in the last year of his life; because he left half his estate and a four-hundred-volume library to the newly founded college at Cambridge, the school was named in his honor

Nathaniel Hawthorne (1804-1864), born in Salem; novelist; often depicted the Puritan New England of the 1600s in his sketches, tales, and novels; best known for *The Scarlet Letter* and *The House of the Seven Gables*

Oliver Wendell Holmes (1809-1894), born in Cambridge; physician, educator, and author; Harvard Medical School professor for more than thirty years and its dean for six years; helped launch the magazine *Atlantic Monthly*; turned his first twelve *Atlantic Monthly* columns into the book *The Autocrat of the Breakfast Table*

Oliver Wendell Holmes, Jr. (1841-1935), born in Boston, son of Oliver Wendell Holmes; jurist; associate justice (1882-99) and chief justice (1899-1902) of the Massachusetts supreme court; associate justice of the United States Supreme Court (1902-32); wrote the classic legal text *The Common Law*

FELIX FRANKFURTER

WM. LLOYD GARRISON

NATHANIEL HAWTHORNE

OLIVER W. HOLMES

JULIA WARD HOWE

HENRY JAMES

WILLIAM JAMES

JOHN F. KENNEDY

Winslow Homer (1836-1910), born in Boston; artist; apprentice to a Boston lithographer; opened his own studio and became known especially for his dramatic seascapes

Julia Ward Howe (1819-1910); author, lecturer, and social reformer; worked in Massachusetts for abolition, world peace, and woman suffrage; wrote the text of "The Battle Hymn of the Republic"

Samuel Gridley Howe (1801-1876), born in Boston; social reformer, educator, and abolitionist; with wife Julia Ward Howe, published the anti-slavery paper *The Commonwealth*; worked to improve education, especially for the handicapped; founder of the Perkins Institute for the Blind

Henry James (1843-1916); novelist; explored the effect of sophisticated European manners and culture on "innocent" Americans; claimed Cambridge as his American home although he settled in England and became a British citizen; noted works include *Daisy Miller, The Portrait of a Lady*, and *The Bostonians*

William James (1842-1910); psychologist, philosopher; brother of Henry James; Harvard professor of anatomy, physiology, and philosophy (1872-1907); set up the first psychological laboratory in America; his beliefs became the basis for a philosophical movement called pragmatism

Edward Moore (Ted) Kennedy (1932-   ), born in Boston; politician; brother of President John F. Kennedy; United States senator (1962-   ); chairman of the Senate's Judiciary Committee (1979-81); unsuccessful candidate for the Democratic Party presidential nomination (1980)

John Fitzgerald Kennedy (1917-1963), born in Brookline; thirty-fifth President of the United States (1961-1963); United States representative (1947-53), United States senator (1953-60); Democrat who worked for social-welfare programs, civil-rights legislation, and the first manned space flights; in 1961 established the United States Peace Corps; sponsored ill-fated "Bay of Pigs" invasion to overthrow Cuba's Fidel Castro; sent United States troops to Vietnam as "advisers"; helped bring about a "thaw" in cold war relations after he avoided the threat of atomic war with the Soviet Union while forcing the removal of Russian missiles from Cuba; assassinated by Lee Harvey Oswald in Dallas, Texas in 1963

Joseph Patrick Kennedy (1888-1969), born in Boston; businessman, diplomat; patriarch of a family that remained at the forefront of American politics throughout most of the twentieth century; first chairman of the Securities and Exchange Commission (1934-35); United States ambassador to Great Britain (1937-40)

Robert Francis Kennedy (1925-1968), born in Brookline, lawyer, politician; brother of President John F. Kennedy; United States attorney general (1961-64); represented New York in the United States Senate (1965-68); assassinated in 1968 while campaigning in Los Angeles for Democratic party presidential nomination

Serge Koussevitzky (1874-1951); Russian-born conductor; principal conductor of the Boston Symphony Orchestra (1924-49)

SERGE KOUSSEVITZKY

Henry Cabot Lodge (1850-1924), born in Boston; historian and politician; United States representative (1887-93); United States senator (1894-1924); in 1919, as chairman of the Senate Foreign Relations Committee, fought successfully to keep the United States from participating in the League of Nations

Henry Cabot Lodge, Jr. (1902-1985), born in Nahant; politician and diplomat; United States senator (1937-53); United States chief delegate to the United Nations (1953-60); ambassador to South Vietnam (1963-64, 1965-67); chief negotiator for the United States at the 1969 Vietnam peace talks in Paris

Henry Wadsworth Longfellow (1807-1882), born in Portland, Maine (then part of Massachusetts); most famous and best-loved American poet of the nineteenth century; Harvard professor (1843-82); used themes from American history in the narrative poems *Evangeline, Song of Hiawatha*, and *The Courtship of Miles Standish*, as well as in the popular short poems "The Village Blacksmith" and "Paul Revere's Ride"

HENRY CABOT LODGE

Amy Lowell (1874-1925), born in Brookline; poet, critic, lecturer; wrote in the style known as free verse; posthumously awarded the 1926 Pulitzer Prize in poetry for *What's O'Clock*

Francis Cabot Lowell (1775-1817), born in Newburyport; industrialist; founded the textile industry in the United States by establishing at Waltham the first mill to put all the stages of cotton-cloth manufacturing under one roof; designed America's first planned industrial city

Robert Lowell (1917-1977), born in Boston; poet; received the Pulitzer Prize in poetry for *Lord Weary's Castle* (1947) and for *The Dolphin* (1974)

AMY LOWELL

Mary Lyon (1797-1849), born near Buckland; educator; in 1837 founded the first women's college in the country, Mount Holyoke Female Seminary (later renamed Mount Holyoke College)

Horace Mann (1769-1859), born in Franklin; educator considered the father of American public education; led the fight for free, universal education; helped create the Massachusetts State Board of Education; United States representative (1848-53)

John Phillips Marquand (1893-1960); novelist; wrote social satires that pointed to the decay of Boston's aristocrats; won the 1938 Pulitzer Prize in fiction for *The Late George Apley*

HORACE MANN

COTTON MATHER

THOMAS O'NEILL

WENDELL PHILLIPS

PAUL REVERE

Massasoit (1580-1661), Wampanoag chief; loyal friend of the Pilgrims; in 1621 made a peace treaty with the Pilgrims and maintained peaceful relations with them throughout his life; in return for his help and friendship, the Pilgrims invited him and his people to a feast that became known as the first Thanksgiving

Cotton Mather (1663-1728), born in Boston; Congregational minister of Boston's North Church (1685-1728); noted scholar who wrote over four hundred works on theology, science, and New England history; was widely criticized by the public for his support of smallpox inoculation

Samuel McIntire (1757-1811); born in Salem; architect, craftsman; designed much of the colonial architecture of Salem

Metacom (King Philip) (1639?-1676); Wampanoag chief; son of Massasoit; in 1675, in response to continuing white encroachment upon Indian lands, began the raids on English settlers that became known as King Philip's War

Thomas Philip (Tip) O'Neill (1912-   ), born in Cambridge; Democratic politician; member of the Massachusetts General Court (1936-51); United States representative (1952-86); Speaker of the House (1977-87); became one of the most powerful and influential figures in Congress

Wendell Phillips (1811-1884), born in Boston, orator and reformer; crusaded for the abolition of slavery; president of the Anti-Slavery Society (1865-70); when the slavery issue was resolved, turned his attention to support of woman suffrage, penal reform, trade unions, and temperance

Sylvia Plath (1932-1963), born in Boston; poet; her troubled life was reflected in her poems and in her suicide at the age of thirty; won the 1982 Pulitzer Prize in poetry for *The Collected Poems*, published after her death

Paul Revere (1735-1818), born in Boston; patriot, silversmith; made a famous ride to warn the countryside that British troops were coming; cast bronze cannon and learned to manufacture gunpowder for the war; designed and printed the first issue of Continental paper money; designed the Massachusetts state seal; built the first copper-rolling mill in the United States

Henry Hobson Richardson (1836-1886), architect; noted for helping to develop a truly American style of architecture; important works include Trinity Church in Boston and Sever and Austin halls at Harvard University in Cambridge

Samoset (1590?-1653?), Pemaquid Indian leader; spoke English and became a loyal friend of the Pilgrims; introduced the English settlers to Massasoit

Anne Sexton (1928-1974), born in Newton; poet; Boston University professor (1970-72); used details of her own life in much of her poetry; won the 1967 Pulitzer Prize in poetry for *Live or Die*

Squanto, or **Tisquantum** (1585?-1622), born near Plymouth; Patuxet Indian; was captured by an English expedition and sold as a slave in Spain; learned English after escaping to England; in 1619 made his way back to America; served as an interpreter for the Plymouth Colony settlers during negotiations with Massasoit; taught the settlers how to plant corn and where to find game and fish

Lucy Stone (1818-1893), born near West Brookfield; abolitionist and pioneer in women's rights; in 1850, in Worcester, helped organize the first national convention on women's rights; in 1869 organized the American Woman Suffrage Association

LUCY STONE

Henry David Thoreau (1817-1862), born in Concord; essayist, naturalist, and philosopher; was associated with the transcendentalists; stressed the right of the individual to refuse to obey government laws in his 1849 essay "Civil Disobedience"; put his transcendentalist ideas into practice by isolating himself at Walden Pond near Concord, where he devoted himself to writing and studying nature; recounted his experience in *Walden*

David Walker (1785-1830); abolitionist; settled in Boston in 1827; contributor to *Freedom's Journal*, the first black newspaper in the United States; leader in the anti-slavery Colored Association; wrote the strongest antislavery statement by any black author of the time in the pamphlet *Appeal to the Colored Citizens of the World*

HENRY D. THOREAU

Daniel Webster (1782-1852); lawyer and statesman; was the most famous orator of his time; advocate of a strong national government; United States representatives (1823-27); United States senator (1827-41, 1845-50); secretary of state under presidents Harrison, Tyler, and Fillmore

Phillis Wheatley (1753?-1784); poet; as a child was kidnaped from Africa and taken to Boston as a slave; at the age of eight was sold as a family servant to Boston tailor John Wheatley who encouraged her education; began writing poetry at the age of thirteen; became the first important black American poet

DANIEL WEBSTER

James Abbott McNeill Whistler (1834-1903), born in Lowell; artist; produced his major works after 1855, when he moved to Europe; best known for his *Arrangement in Gray and Black No. 1: Portrait of the Artist's Mother*, popularly called *Whistler's Mother*

John Greenleaf Whittier (1807-1892), born near Haverhill; poet; known as the "Quaker Poet"; recounted life in the American colonies and in his boyhood New England; also wrote newspaper articles and poems supporting the antislavery movement

John Winthrop (1588-1649); Puritan leader; first governor of the Massachusetts Bay Colony; served as governor and in other administrative positions until his death; led the colony through its first hard winter and into prosperity

JOHN WINTHROP

131

GOVERNORS

John Hancock	1780-1785	George D. Robinson	1884-1887
James Bowdoin	1785-1787	Oliver Ames	1887-1890
John Hancock	1787-1793	James Q. A. Brackett	1890-1891
Samuel Adams	1793-1797	William E. Russell	1891-1894
Increase Sumner	1797-1800	Frederic T. Greenhalge	1894-1896
Caleb Strong	1800-1807	Roger Wolcott	1896-1900
James Sullivan	1807-1809	Winthrop M. Crane	1900-1903
Levi Lincoln	1809	John L. Bates	1903-1905
Christopher Gore	1809-1810	William L. Douglas	1905-1906
Elbridge Gerry	1810-1812	Curtis Guild, Jr.	1906-1909
Caleb Strong	1812-1816	Eben S. Draper	1909-1911
John Brooks	1816-1823	Eugene N. Foss	1911-1914
William Eustis	1823-1825	David I. Walsh	1914-1916
Marcus Morton	1825	Samuel W. McCall	1916-1919
Levi Lincoln	1825-1834	Calvin Coolidge	1919-1921
John Davis	1834-1835	Channing H. Cox	1921-1925
Samuel Armstrong	1835-1836	Alvin T. Fuller	1925-1929
Edward Everett	1836-1840	Frank G. Allen	1929-1931
Marcus Morton	1840-1841	Joseph B. Ely	1931-1935
John Davis	1841-1843	James M. Curley	1935-1937
Marcus Morton	1843-1844	Charles F. Hurley	1937-1939
George N. Briggs	1844-1851	Leverett Saltonstall	1939-1945
George S. Boutwell	1851-1853	Maurice J. Tobin	1945-1947
John H. Clifford	1853-1854	Robert F. Bradford	1947-1949
Emory Washburn	1854-1855	Paul A. Dever	1949-1953
Henry J. Gardner	1855-1858	Christian A. Herter	1953-1957
Nathaniel P. Banks	1858-1861	Foster Furcolo	1957-1961
John A. Andrew	1861-1866	John A. Volpe	1961-1963
Alexander H. Bullock	1866-1869	Endicott Peabody	1963-1965
William Claflin	1869-1872	John A. Volpe	1965-1969
William B. Washburn	1872-1874	Francis Sargent	1969-1975
Thomas Talbot	1874-1875	Michael S. Dukakis	1975-1979
William Gaston	1875-1876	Edward J. King	1979-1983
Alexander H. Rice	1876-1879	Michael S. Dukakis	1983-1991
Thomas Talbot	1879-1880	William Weld	1991-
John D. Long	1880-1883		
Benjamin F. Butler	1883-1884		

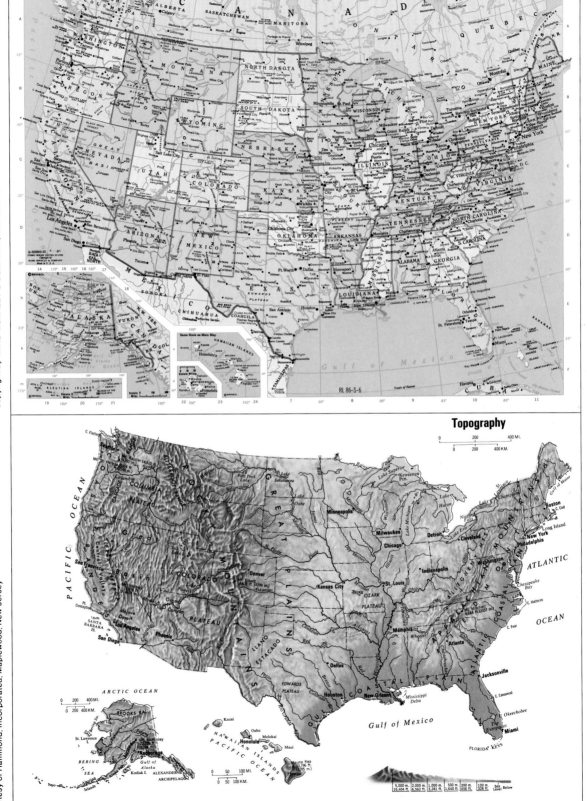

Topography

MAP KEY

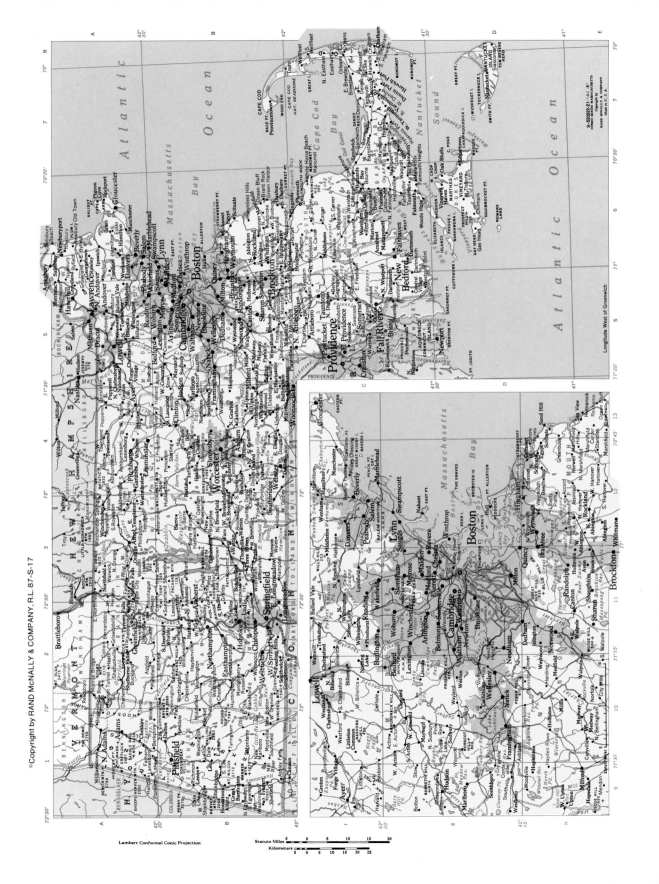

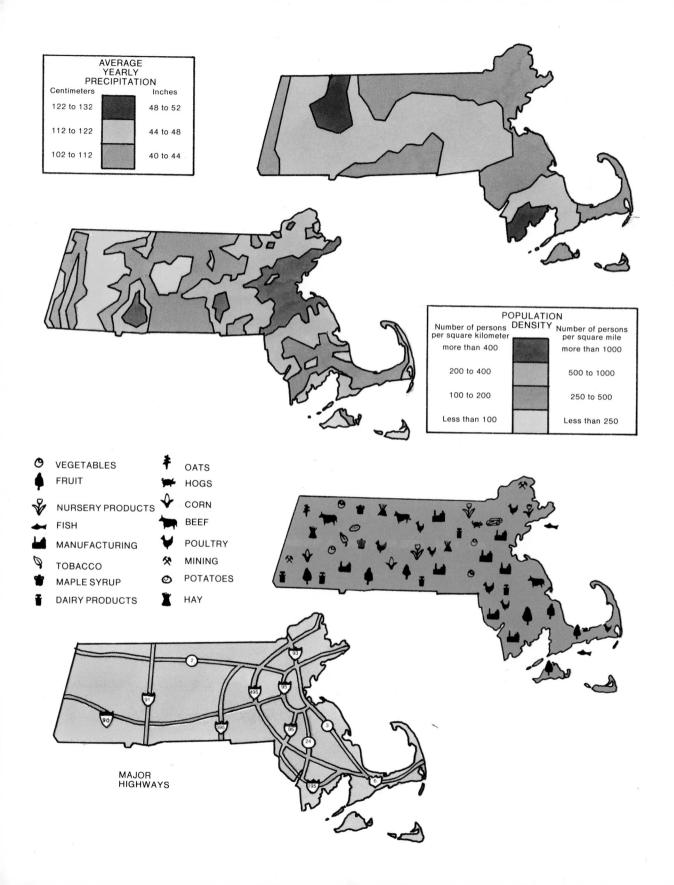

AVERAGE
YEARLY
PRECIPITATION

Centimeters | Inches

122 to 132 | 48 to 52

112 to 122 | 44 to 48

102 to 112 | 40 to 44

POPULATION DENSITY

Number of persons per square kilometer | Number of persons per square mile

more than 400 | more than 1000

200 to 400 | 500 to 1000

100 to 200 | 250 to 500

Less than 100 | Less than 250

VEGETABLES
FRUIT
NURSERY PRODUCTS
FISH
MANUFACTURING
TOBACCO
MAPLE SYRUP
DAIRY PRODUCTS

OATS
HOGS
CORN
BEEF
POULTRY
MINING
POTATOES
HAY

MAJOR
HIGHWAYS

TOPOGRAPHY

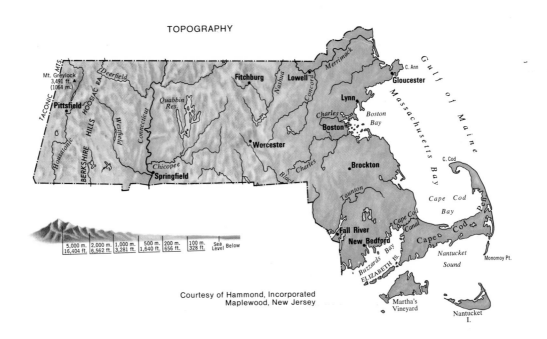

Mt. Greylock
3,491 ft.
(1064 m.)

TACONIC MTS.

Pittsfield

Deerfield

BERKSHIRE HILLS

HOOSAC RA.

Housatonic

Westfield

Connecticut

Quabbin Res.

Chicopee

Springfield

Fitchburg

Nashua

Lowell

Merrimack

Concord

Worcester

Charles

Black

Charles

Lynn

Boston

Brockton

Taunton

Fall River

New Bedford

Cape Cod Canal

Buzzards Bay

ELIZABETH IS.

Cape Cod

Nantucket Sound

Monomoy Pt.

Martha's Vineyard

Nantucket I.

C. Ann

Gloucester

Gulf of Maine

Massachusetts Bay

Boston Bay

C. Cod

Cape Cod Bay

5,000 m. 16,404 ft. | 2,000 m. 6,562 ft. | 1,000 m. 3,281 ft. | 500 m. 1,640 ft. | 200 m. 656 ft. | 100 m. 328 ft. | Sea Level | Below

Courtesy of Hammond, Incorporated
Maplewood, New Jersey

COUNTIES

BERKSHIRE

Pittsfield

FRANKLIN

Greenfield

HAMPSHIRE

Northampton

HAMPDEN

Springfield

WORCESTER

Worcester

ESSEX

Salem

MIDDLESEX

Cambridge

SUFFOLK

BOSTON

Dedham

NORFOLK

PLYMOUTH

Plymo.

Taunton

BRISTOL

BARNSTABLE

Barnstable

DUKES

Edgartown

NANTUCKET

Nantucket

View of Boston from across the Charles River

INDEX

Page numbers that appear in boldface indicate illustrations

A Cape Cod sea shack hung with lobstering gear

Picture Identifications

Front cover: Aerial view of Boston showing Beacon Hill and the downtown skyline
Back cover: Rockport
Pages 2-3: The North Bridge in Concord
Page 6: Men dressed in revolutionary war costumes during a parade in Newburyport
Pages 8-9: The Connecticut River near Sunderland
Pages 18-19: Montage of the various types of people who live and work in Massachusetts
Pages 26-27: The landing of the Pilgrims in 1620
Pages 38-39: Boston as it appeared in the mid-eighteenth century
Page 48: Woman working at a loom in a New England textile mill
Page 58: State militia trying to control strikers during the famous 1912 Lawrence textile strike
Page 68: The State House in Boston, Massachusetts' state capitol building
Page 79: Boston's Public Garden
Pages 92-93: Nantucket
Page 93 (inset): Acorn Street on Boston's Beacon Hill
Page 108: Montage showing the state flag, the state bird (chickadee), the state flower (mayflower), the state animal (Morgan horse), and the state tree (American elm)

About the Author

Deborah Kent grew up in New Jersey and received her B.A. from Oberlin College. As a graduate student at Smith College School for Social Work in Northampton, Massachusetts, she spent a year in Boston doing field work at Massachusetts General Hospital. Ms. Kent practiced social work in New York City and taught disabled children in Mexico before embarking on a full-time career as a freelance writer.

Deborah Kent is the author of eleven novels for young adults, as well as numerous articles and book reviews. She lives in Chicago with her husband and their daughter Janna.

Picture Acknowledgments

The Image Bank: ©Steve Proehl: Front cover
H. Armstrong Roberts, Inc.: Pages 45, 124 (both photos), 125 (Bryant), 126 (Coolidge, Eddy), 128 (Howe, H. James),129 (Mann), 130 (Mather, Revere), 131 (Thoreau, Webster, Winthrop); ©A. Griffin: Pages 2-3, 79, 92-93; ©G. Ahrens: Pages 8-9; ©J. Blank: Pages 13 (left), 105, 107; ©Ralph Krubner: Page 73 (bottom left)
Marilyn Gartman Agency: ©Michael Philip Manheim: Pages 4, 18 (bottom right), 35 (right), 88 (left), 93 (inset), 99, 103 (top)
©**Steve Lipofsky:** Pages 5, 19 (top right), 91 (left)
©**Robert Frerck/Odyssey Productions:** Pages 6, 19, (middle left, bottom right), 73 (top right), 78 (both photos), 97, 102, 120, 121
Tom Stack & Associates: ©Alan D. Briere: Page 86 (bottom left); ©Don & Pat Valenti: Back cover
©**Lynn M. Stone:** Pages 11 (right), 112, 141
Nawrocki Stock Photo: ©Jeff Apoian: Page 13 (right); ©Ted Cordingly: Pages 16 (right), 74; ©Jerry Howard: Page 19 (center); ©Robert Perron: Page 73 (top left)
©**Joseph A. DiChello, Jr.:** Pages 15, 19 (top left, bottom left), 21
©**Owen Franken:** Pages 16 (left), 73 (bottom right)
R/C Agency: ©Richard L. Capps: Page 18 (top left, bottom left)
©**Renee DeKona:** Page 18 (top right)
Journalism Services: ©Mike Kidulich: Page 18 (center); ©Tim McCabe: Page 101 (right)
Stock Boston: ©Richard Pasley: Page 11 (left); ©Herb Snitzer Photography: Page 19 (middle right); ©Paul Mozell: Page 77 (left); ©James R. Holland: Page 89; ©Julie Houck: Page 90; ©John Coletti: Page 91 (right); ©Lionel Delevingne: Page 95
Photosynthesis: ©Russell Schleipman: Page 23 (left), 88 (right), 138; ©David Edward Dempster: Page 117
John F. Kennedy Library: Page 23 (right)
Roloc Color Slides: Pages 26-27, 46 (both photos), 50 (left), 68, 98, 103 (bottom)
Historical Pictures Service, Inc., Chicago: Pages 31, 32, 33, 35 (left), 36 (right), 41 (all photos), 42 (both photos), 43, 48, 50 (right), 54, 55, 81, 82 (left), 86 (top left, top right), 125 (Alcott, Brandeis), 126 (Dickinson, DuBois), 127 (Frankfurter, Hawthorne, Holmes), 128 (W. James), 129 (Koussevitzky, Lodge, Lowell), 130 (Phillips), 131 (Stone)
North Wind Picture Archives: Page 36 (left)
Photri: Pages 38-39, 71, 82 (right), 83 (right), 108 (top left, tree), 125 (Anthony), 127 (Garrison), 128 (Kennedy), 130 (O'Neill); ©Dr. C. W. Biedel: Page 96
The Bettmann Archive: Pages 52, 58, 60, 63 (top left, top right, bottom left)
UPI/Bettmann: Pages 63 (bottom right), 66 (both photos)
Root Resources: ©Jack Monsarratt: Page 77 (right)
©**Mary Ann Brockman:** Pages 83 (left), 119
©**Virginia Grimes:** Page 86 (bottom right)
©**The Photo Source:** Page 101 (left)
©**Reinhard Brucker:** Page 108 (bottom left)
©**James P. Rowan:** Page 108 (top right)
Len W. Meents: Maps on Pages 95, 96, 98, 103, 105, 136
Courtesy Flag Research Center, Winchester, Massachusetts 01890: Flag on page 108